Prepare for Opportunity

A Practical Guide for Applying for a Job in Sports

Kelley K. Walton

Kendall Hunt
publishing company

Cover image © 2013 Shutterstock, Inc.

www.kendallhunt.com
Send all inquiries to:
4050 Westmark Drive
Dubuque, IA 52004-1840

Printed in the United States of America
10 9 8 7 6 5 4 3 2 1

"A successful team beats with one heart"

- Unknown

This book is dedicated to Team Walton.
You three truly are Triple Trouble.
I love you guys!

Table of Contents   Page

-Introduction-

For seven of my ten years working in professional sports, I was the Director of Human Resources for a major league professional sports team, the Columbus Blue Jackets of the National Hockey League. Which means I did *a lot* of recruiting. Especially recruiting recent college graduates. I was the person, or at least the type of person, on the other side of your online or mailed-in job application.

Each year as the Director of HR, I would attend between four and eight career fairs, meeting hundreds of college students who wanted to work in sports. And every year at the end of career fair season, I would feel compelled to write a book for applicants that provided advice for those applying for a job in sports. I felt that whether they were either getting bad advice or they weren't accepting the good advice that had been given; they were sorely unprepared for the job application process in the sport industry.

Most applicants I have encountered aren't lacking intelligence, talent or even ability. However, many are lacking self-awareness, especially as it compares to other applicants and the heavy competition for the job; confidence in explaining why they should be considered by our company for employment; and their surroundings, including the fact that they have generally 2-3 minutes to make a good impression at career fairs and that it *can* actually lead to an interview that can lead to an internship or a job. They are also severely lacking in both their presentation of their own knowledge, skills and abilities and in their understanding of the companies that they are applying with. Overall, many people were generally unprepared for how to *successfully* apply for a job in sports.

Now, not everyone I have come across is a terrible job applicant. I've hired some tremendous talent over the years. I am proud to have been a part of the start up era of an expansion team and I am proud to have worked with some incredibly talented and successful people over the years. However, it is the vast number of unprepared applicants that I've encountered that has prompted me to write this book.

While most of my recruiting experience has been in professional sports and this book is geared toward those applying for a job in the sport industry, the material is applicable to any industry, as the job

1

application procedures are similar, especially for jobs with a high volume of applicants. So, if you are applying for jobs either in or out of the sport industry, most of this advice will apply. It also is meant mainly for college students or recent college graduates. But that doesn't mean this book won't be helpful to others who are looking for a change in career or who just need a refresher in the job application process.

The goal of this book is to provide some advice that will give you a leg up on the competition. Keep in mind, however, that the key to your success is what you do with the advice. *You* will need to do the work to make the most of your opportunities.

-Chapter 1: Working in Sports -

"Many of us spend half our time wishing for things we could have,
if we didn't spend half our time wishing."
Alexander Woollcott

Sports is a highly competitive industry. And not just on the field, court, ice, etc. There are over 250 Sports Management academic programs in the United States that produce thousands of new graduates each year. It isn't a requirement to study Sports Management (or Sports Administration, Sports Marketing, Sport Industry, etc.) to work in the Sport Industry, so those graduates with a Sports related degree are competing with applicants who have degrees in a variety of areas – business, management, communications, marketing, and journalism, to name a few. And vice versa. Graduates in marketing, journalism and business are competing with applicants who have studied the business of sports and (should) have an understanding of the unique business of sports.

There are a lot of areas that encompass "sports management". There are classes and programs that can provide you with much more detail about what this area of study is. However, in brief, Sport Management typically includes the study of management, marketing, sales, facility management, professional sports, college athletics, finance, and law as it relates to the business of sport.

The business of sports is unique, there is no doubt. Unlike traditional industries like oil, wireless communications, or consumer goods; sport teams must both cooperate and compete, they are extremely dependent on the media, and they have to deal with consumers who think they are experts. Can you imagine if someone proposed that Verizon should share revenue with AT&T to ensure its viability in the industry? Or vice versa? No. But many professional sports leagues have some form of revenue sharing to ensure that smaller market or smaller revenue generating teams are viable. Have you ever heard of someone calling up the President of Procter & Gamble to tell them that the pH levels in Tide are too high? I doubt it. And if so, I doubt it's a regular occurrence. But often fans of sports teams believe that they have not only a right to complain to upper management, but that they have the solution to the team's latest losing streak. Managing a product that is unpredictable and tied to emotions makes it a unique business to manage and therefore it is important to understand the unique approaches in marketing, business, finance, etc.

College sports will vary depending on a variety of factors, including the Division Level and the revenue generated by the athletic programs. Professional sports will vary depending on a variety of factors, including the type of sport being played, the amount of money available for revenue sharing, and whether there is a Collective Bargaining Agreement that outlines how much revenue the players get versus how much the owners have to operate the business (and/or make profit). While many principles run true throughout the industry, working as a marketing professional in the National Football League is going to be different from working as a marketing professional for a Single A Baseball Team. Both can give you excellent experience, but the way you would approach your marketing plans are going to be different – different budgets, different target markets, different market competition, etc.

Now, I'm going to leave the questions of "where to work" and what kind of positions you are qualified to other resources. There are plenty of resources out there to help you with those questions. Some resources are listed at the end of this book in Appendix D: Recommended Resources. This book is not designed for that. This book is designed for the person who already has some idea of the career path that they wish to pursue and to assist you in applying for that job. Whether you want to work for a league office, professional sport team (NFL, NHL, NBA, MLB, NASCAR, MLS, Minor League Professional Sports, etc.), Sport/Team Operations (General Managers, Coaches, Scouts), Business Operations (Marketing, Sales, Public Relations, etc.), Administrative Operations (Legal, Finance, Information Technology, Human Resources), or Facility Management; or whether you want to work in College Athletics which can also be broken down in a variety of ways from the University levels and Conference levels and from Athletic Directors and Coaches to Marketing and Facility Management; or whether you want to work in any of the other Sport Industry segments like Amateur Athletics, Sports Marketing Agencies, merchandise, equipment and apparel or the like. I will leave those choices up to you and the good resources that are available to you to determine that.

I can tell you from personal experience and from working with others in the sport industry that working in sports is fun. It is a unique experience. You get a satisfaction from being a part of something that is "special" or "exciting," but there is also a tremendous personal commitment that you make when you work in sports. It is important to know that the time demands do not always equal the pay that goes with a position. With that said, I'm not sure there are many other industries that provide the job satisfaction that working in sports does. And obviously, there is a large draw to work in sports, hence the heavy competition for jobs. However, I encourage each person applying for a job in sports to understand some very basic information: You are applying for a JOB with a BUSINESS. Be professional. Be prepared. Understand that it isn't fun and games all day long. It's actual work. It's a business that sells something fun – sports and entertainment. But it is still a business.

-Chapter 2: Résumés-

We judge ourselves by what we feel capable of doing,
while others judge us by what we have already done.
Longfellow

A résumé is a brief summary of education, experience, and skills that is prepared by an applicant for a job. Note that it should be **BRIEF**. For those just graduating from college, keep it to one page. For anyone, it should *never* be longer than three pages. If so, you have gone well beyond a *brief* description of your qualifications for the job.

While there are various types of résumés out there, I'm going to give you one very basic template. You can use this for any position. And you can choose your own font or style if you would like to change it up a bit. You can add your own personal touch. That is fine. If you want variety, there are plenty of good résumé examples out there. I have included some examples in Appendix E. From a recruiter/employer perspective – **content is more important than format.**

As you begin the process of developing a résumé and cover letter for your job hunting, it is important to keep in mind the following goals:

The goal of the cover letter is to get the reader to read your résumé.

The goal of the résumé is to get you an interview.

The goal of the interview is to get you the job.

I think it is also very important to remember that it isn't a résumé that gets you the job. It is the professional manner in which you present a summary of your experiences. Those experiences need to match the job opening that you are being considered for. Said a little bit better...

What gets you an interview ...
- **a professional, concise résumé**
- **that outlines your experience**
- **that matches the open position requirements and**
- **outweighs the other candidates who have applied for the position.**

It's not snappy. It's not clever. However, it is the truth. It's a simple concept – but it is the heart of job attainment.

Many people want someone else to write their résumé. There are several résumé services out there who will do this for you – for a fee. Some of them are quite good. However, I would argue that you are doing yourself a disservice if you aren't heavily involved in the résumé creation process. If you can't write your own résumé, how in the world are you going to succeed in an interview? If you can't summarize your education, knowledge and skills in a page or two, how are you going to spend 30 minutes, 2 hours or a half-day (depending on the process) interviewing for a position? If nothing else, the résumé is your practice for preparing your sales pitch that you are the best candidate for the job.

You will find that some of the advice in this book is extremely picky and very much about the details. It isn't because employers are sitting around trying to find some way to weed out applicants (well... some employers may be doing that). I have found over and over that the difference between good and great is in the details. And that's what employers are looking for. Employers are looking for great applicants. Employers are looking for applicants who show a promise of intelligence and an ability to communicate professionally. That is why the details of a résumé make all the difference.

It is important for applicants to know that in highly competitive positions, there are employers who will not consider applicants who have spelling or grammar mistakes. By not proofreading your résumé and cover letter, you are telling the employer you really aren't as interested in the position as others who submit résumés without error. As well, employers need to trust that if they hire you, the business communication that you will send out on the company's behalf will be professional and correct. The easiest way to screen for this ability is a cover letter and résumé. And in a highly competitive job market, employers can be picky.

First and Most Important Step

You have to care. I'm Captain Obvious on this one, right? But if you don't care enough to ensure that your application is professional, correct, and up to date; why should the company care about hiring you? Misspellings, improper grammar, or addressing your cover letter to the wrong person – these things all indicate to the employer that you don't really care. So if you don't care, why should they?

Résumé Basics:

- Use 10, 11 or 12-point font.
- Use a business-type font (Garamond, **Times New Roman**, **Calibri**, **Georgia** or similar professional style font)
- Keep the font the same throughout the entire résumé. You may want to make your name 1 or 2 points larger font than the rest – but that's it. Keep it all the same size. You can bold, underline and italicize for effect. But do not change the font for effect.
- Single-space your résumé. (Yes – even if it makes it look short).
- Make sure your résumé is the proper length. There are résumé experts out there who will claim that for a college graduate it MUST be only one page. However, I've seen résumés for college graduates that were *appropriately* 1½ or 2 pages. My best advice on this is that if your résumé is more than one page and you have less than three years of post-graduate experience, make sure that you don't have irrelevant information in your résumé that is going to make the potential employer say "Wow. This person is full of crap." That will not get your résumé moving in the right direction through the process. Employers see right through large font, double spaced résumés that are trying to make it seem like applicants have more experience than they do. Bottom line: if your résumé is more than a page, use a lower point font, single space and rework your wording to make sure whether your résumé is appropriately more than a page. Remember, it should be brief.
- Use proper tense throughout. For past positions, you should use past tense and for current positions you should use present tense. Double check to make sure for a past position you don't write "responsible for overseeing…" and then on the next line write "conducted training sessions." And don't write "prepared financial information" and then "creating spreadsheets." Tense is important. It is basic grammar. Employers will expect you to have basic grammar skills.
  - If you do not understand tense, go read *The McGraw-Hill Handbook of English Grammar and Usage* by Mark Lester and Larry Beason. Again, basic grammar is knowledge employers would expect you to possess.
- If you have a GPA above a 3.0 on a 4.0 scale, you should list your GPA. For some employers it is a must. For many employers it is only one of many factors.

- Use one phone number. Use the number you want the potential employer to use to call you. Do not expect an employer to "track you down." Leave one number that you will either answer when they call or one that has a voicemail that you check regularly.
- Have a professional voicemail announcement for when a potential employer calls. Remember that you are entering the world of professionals. You want to come across like a professional.

> PROFESSIONAL: "You have reached the voicemail of Mark Davis. I am unable to answer your call. Please leave a message and I will return your call as soon as possible. Thank you."

> PROFESSIONAL: "You've reached the voicemail of Mark Davis. I am unavailable. Please leave a message and I'll get back to you shortly."

> NOT PROFESSIONAL: "You've reached Mark, you know what to do."

> NOT PROFESSIONAL: "Yo. Leave it."

Will a not so professional message deter employers from bringing you in to interview? Maybe. Maybe not. But why risk it? My goal here is to increase your chances. And having a professional voicemail increases those chances.

- Have a professional email address.

> PROFESSIONAL: yourname9@whatever.com

> NOT PROFESSIONAL: partygirl@whatever.com

> NOT PROFESSIONAL: kegsrus920@whatever.com

Beyond the Basics:

Do not put your picture on your résumé. This seems to be a recent trend. If you are an attractive person, it certainly doesn't hurt to showcase that, but rarely does your personality come across in a picture. It often gives the impression of arrogance and should be avoided, unless you are applying for a job where your attractiveness is a major factor in hiring, for example a spirit/dance team, modeling, or a position in television or video that makes appearance relevant. If you feel absolutely compelled to put a picture on your résumé or as an attachment in an email application, you <u>must</u> use a professional photo. Do not use a photo of yourself at a social event. (Yes – I have seen this on a résumé). Also, there are several areas of the law that you may not be thinking of during the hiring process, but as an HR professional, I am. In order to avoid discriminatory practices, most HR professionals go to great lengths to ensure that the hiring managers don't know the gender, race, religion, etc. of the applicant. By putting your picture on the résumé, you've just made that part of the HR professional's job much harder.

I do not recommend a career summary, objective statement; project summary or career highlights section. If you have over eight years of varied work experience, it might make sense for a career summary. Otherwise, these add bulk to your résumé and most employers do not find them useful. You are applying for a job or internship and they know that your objective is to land that job or interview. I have seen résumés that have a short statement: "Objective: to obtain the open position of Inside Sales Representative." That works just fine. But if you're going to add an objective statement, it should be tailored to the employer, and that is better left to the cover letter, not the résumé. Many (and yes I mean many) people forget to make the changes. This is often the first line an employer reads about you. It is often your first impression. Make it a good one. If you feel that you must use an objective statement, keep it simple. But I don't know any recruiter who requires objective statements in considering applicants. It is an unnecessary statement that doesn't do much for your chances. I recommend leaving it off.

If you are a recent college graduate, it helps to put a listing of relevant college courses (business courses, sport management/administration, sport marketing, etc.) and/or major college projects. Some employers may not be familiar with certain majors and having a short listing of relevant classes may be helpful to understand what classes you have taken that may be relevant to the position you are applying for. I recommend having a two to three column section for this. You don't want it to take up too much space on your résumé, but it is something that provides more detail about your education that the title of your major alone won't provide. It can help an employer understand what classes you've taken to prepare for the position you are applying for. Employers may not understand what a "Communications Major" or "Strategic Communications Major" or "Management Major" entails. Showing them a list of classes can be an asset.

I get a lot of questions about whether or not to leave high school information on your résumé. My take is that if you are two years or less removed from high school, it's probably acceptable to keep your high school information on your résumé. Otherwise, keep only significant accomplishments and/or activities on the résumé. Some work experience may be relevant, but by the time you are a junior in college, you should have enough other relevant experience (work experience, internships, organization involvement, etc.) that will be more important to potential employers.

I have seen a recent trend to make résumés accomplishment driven. I disagree with this advice. Like many things, it may not keep you from getting the job or interview. And obviously, an employer wants to know your accomplishments. However, more than anything else, employers are trying to get a sense of what your work experience is compared with the job description and compared against other applicants. They want to know what were the jobs you held and what did you do in those jobs (responsibilities). Accomplishments are important to list under the jobs held. However, résumés should *not* be accomplishment driven. Accomplishment driven résumés make it more difficult to compare an applicant to the job posting and to other candidates. You want to make it as easy as possible for them to see how you meet their expectations.

Stay away from "never," "all," "ever," "always," and "about". Instead of about, use approximate or approximately. For the others, you most likely don't need the adverb.

Don't "oversell" yourself or what you did in a position. If you were a receptionist and your job was to answer and route calls and greet guests, then leave it at that. When people try to overstate their position, potential employers see right through it. For example, if you were a receptionist don't write "provided assistance to clients, resulting in increased sales," unless you can be specific of what revenue you generated. If you are a receptionist for a salon and you tell a client they should get the "color friendly" shampoo for color-treated hair, you didn't increase sales. You provided information. You may have been of some assistance in the process, but don't oversell it. Keep it to the good experience that you do have. For example, that same receptionist may have answered calls, greeted guests and maintained a schedule for the staff. Any of those three skills may be something a potential employer is looking for – phone skills, customer service skills or scheduling.

Explain the product line or business segment when listing previous employers. While some companies are self-explanatory, others are not. If you are applying for a position with a National Basketball Association (NBA) team, do not assume the hiring manager knows that the Single-A affiliate of the Cleveland Indians is the Mahoning Valley Scrappers. If you were an intern for the Mahoning Valley Scrappers, then list it as Mahoning Valley Scrappers, Single-A baseball club affiliate of the Cleveland Indians. If you are applying for a position with the NBA and your previous experience is with another NBA team, there is no need to explain the team listed.

Do not tailor your résumé for the job you are applying for (unless you need to add employer information and/or relevant class information). A résumé should be a snapshot of the jobs you've held and the responsibilities and achievements that occurred at that job. Not what you think the employer wants to see. Your responsibilities and achievements shouldn't change based on the job you are applying for. You will rarely know what an employer is and isn't looking for. Experience in one area might be helpful for the open position, but the employer won't know you have that experience because you're trying to tailor your résumé to the employer and what you think they want to see. However, you will be more successful if you tailor your cover letter to explain how your experience matches the posted requirements and not your résumé. Now, you've probably received just the opposite advice. I have heard this a lot from even what I would consider credible sources. However, I wholeheartedly disagree with tailoring your résumé. Unless you are eight or so years out of college and have varied experience, keep it the same. For example, if you have been out of school for 8 years and you have 4 years of sales experience and 4 years of administrative experience and you are applying for a sales job, you might want to play up the sales experience. And vice versa. If you're applying for an administrative position, you might want to play up that angle. In that situation, you're tailoring your explanation of yourself and not trying to guess what an employer wants.

It is also important to know that most employers will not consider an applicant who has the cover letter addressed to the incorrect person, venue, company, team or university. For example, if you are applying for a job at the San Diego Sports Arena, do not state in your opening paragraph how interested you are in obtaining a position at the Staples Center in Los Angeles. It may simply be an oversight as you rush to send résumés to facilities and/or teams. But it shows a lack of attention to detail and a lack of true interest in the facility or team you with whom you are applying. When there are hundreds of applicants for a position, you need to make your résumé stand out in a way that makes it to the top of the pile, not to the first round of "no" responses, or to the trash, in some cases.

Proofread your résumé several times. Use spell check to make sure that your spelling is correct. But keep in mind that spell check won't catch grammatical mistakes or words that are used incorrectly. You will see more in Chapter 3 about avoiding mistakes.

REMEMBER

> **What gets you an interview ...**
> - **a professional, concise résumé**
> - **that outlines your experience**
> - **that matches the open position requirements and**
> - **outweighs the other candidates who have applied for the position.**

Following is a template for a résumé. If you like, you can jazz this up a bit. This is a very basic template. I've seen good résumés that look nicer and more professional. But, again, I don't believe it is the template that gets you the interview. It's the professional manner in which you present your education and experience.

There is no perfect résumé. Because one employer may be wowed by a fancy, colorful résumé and another employer may be turned off by it. Your best bet is to find the most professional way to present yourself in résumé form.

Following is simply a template for you to start building your résumé. There are some examples of different styles in Appendix E, but for now keep the focus on the details, not the style.

Education:

School Name
Degree Awarded (or area of study if not yet graduated)
Date of anticipated graduation, or upcoming graduation or graduation
GPA or Rank
Awards or distinctions (summa cum laude, cum laude, etc.)

Experience:

Company Name
Job Title
Dates
- Responsibilities
- Responsibilities
- Responsibilities

Company Name
Job Title
Dates
- Responsibilities
- Responsibilities
- Responsibilities

Achievements/Awards:
- List of achievements/awards

Activities:
- List any activities/groups/clubs involved with

Skills:
- List any special skills (computer, research, programs, etc.)

Remember....

What gets you an interview ...
- **a professional, concise résumé**
- **that outlines your experience**
- **that matches the open position requirements and**
- **outweighs the other candidates who have applied for the position.**

Your goal is to make sure the employer has all of the necessary information in order to properly evaluate you next to the other candidates applying for the job. Your résumé will stand out more for providing a clear, concise description of your experience than one that has polka dots on it, one that is wrapped around a hockey puck, one that is silk screened on a t-shirt, or one that is stuffed inside a football cleat.

-Chapter 3: Step-by-Step Résumé-

"Opportunity is missed by most people because it is dressed in overalls
and looks like work."
Thomas Edison

As I stated in the beginning, your success will depend on you.
Below is a step-by-step guide. Work it. Re-work it. Make it your calling
card for success.

**STEP 1: Copy/write the résumé template – exactly as it is – on
your computer in Word or a similar program (one that is
compatible with online applications and can be printed easily).
Bold where it is bold. Italicize where it is italicized.**

**STEP 2:   Enter your basic information – name, address,
educational institution, employers, job titles, dates, etc. over the
template information. Start with the most recent job first and list
your experience chronologically. You start with the most recent
and work backwards from there. The most recent should be at the
top. Do not list responsibilities yet.**

Example:
LMNO Company
Intern
May – August 2012

XYZ Company
Marketing Intern
May – August 2011

**STEP 3: List your job responsibilities. Under each of job titles,
list the responsibilities that you had with each position. Do not
assume you know what the potential employer wants to see.
Simply list your responsibilities clearly and in a professional
manner.**

Step 3 tips

<u>Knowing yourself</u>

What you are doing in writing your résumé is putting on paper the education, experience and that you have. So, you need to know yourself well and be able to intelligently explain your education and experience to others. Or asked more simply ... who are you?

Educational background generally includes your formal training and/or education. Education is usually somewhat straightforward. What did you study? Where did you study it? What degree did you obtain? What grade or ranking did you receive? What year did you graduate or do you expect to graduate? What classes did you take?

Experience and skills tend to be what trips people up when it comes to writing a résumé. People know what they have done, but often struggle putting it into words. What you need to do is very concisely provide an account of what your previous internships and jobs were and what you did in those jobs.

It is also important to understand the difference between working or interning so that it will look good on a résumé and working or interning to gain experience. The difference between these two is often lost on applicants. While it is important to get experience so that you can "put it on a résumé," the key factor is *gaining experience* from the work or internship experience so that you have some skill or experience that is valuable to an employer. It's not just about "putting it on a résumé".

For many people, it is difficult to explain their experience in a way that truly conveys their work experience. People often either underestimate or overestimate what they've done. The key in explaining your experience is to use professional, concise, action verbs that describe what your responsibilities were in a job or internship.

Here are a few examples:

Accomplished	Implemented
Administered	Interviewed
Advised	Maintained
Analyzed	Managed
Answered	Operated
Assisted	Organized
Attained	Oversaw
Attended	Participated
Coached	Performed
Compiled	Prepared
Completed	Processed
Coordinated	Provided
Created	Researched
Demonstrated	Responded to
Designed	Responsible for
Developed	Scheduled
Directed	Served
Drafted	Sold
Edited	Supervised
Engaged	Trained
Ensured	Tutored
Established	Volunteered
Executed	Wrote
Founded	

These action verb examples are written in the past tense. Remember to keep your tense proper. For current positions, use present tense. For past positions, use past tense.

The following statements are examples of how to use some of the above words in a professional, concise statement. Again, the difference between good and great is in the details.

- Advised incoming freshmen on campus events, class scheduling and extracurricular activities.
- Assisted Marketing Manager with promotion implementation.
- Assisted with implementing a free lunch program for homeless families.

19

- Assisted in writing press releases and marketing materials for publication.
- Attended National/Regional Sales Conference. (You may want to provide brief detail about the programs and speakers.)
- Coached Little League Baseball team.
- Coached High School Women's Soccer team to Division III State Finals.
- Compiled statistical data on market trends and presented to top management.
- Conducted phone survey regarding customer satisfaction.
- Conducted employment interviews.
- Consolidated databases for better use in marketing and direct mail campaigns.
- Coordinated office supply orders.
- Created and updated client database using customer relationship management software.
- Created monthly community relations newsletter template.
- Created and published news releases for clients.
- Designed promotional materials for marketing campaign.
- Drafted a customer service procedure manual for ABC Company.
- Entered and updated client information in database management system.
- Generated over 200 leads by cold calling and prospecting.
- Interacted and collaborated with students to create and present a consulting project for a non-profit organization.
- Made outbound calls to generate new customers for ABC Company.
- Managed customer lead project to qualify leads for sales staff.
- Organized and developed on-campus training seminars for XYZ product.
- Organized weekly training session for staff.
- Performed community service and organized fundraising efforts for DEF group.
- Prepared invoices for payment.
- Prepared and maintained departmental budget.
- Processed invoices for payment.

- Provided administrative support, including answering phones and directing incoming clients to appropriate staff members.
- Provided assistance to customers, including assisting guests to seat locations and providing guidance on locations within the facility (ex: elevators, first-aid).
- Researched local companies to create proposal letters and financial plans.
- Responded promptly to customer concerns and requests.
- Tracked advertising and media coverage and summarized in a report for clients.
- Trained new employees on policies and sales techniques.

This list and these examples are not the end all, be all for the verbs you could use to describe your experience. This list is provided to get you started thinking and writing about your experience in a professional, business-like manner.

Details, Details, Details

Many applicants will list as a skill: "attention to detail," yet their résumé has several small mistakes. There are managers who throw out résumés with very small mistakes. It certainly doesn't fast track you to the top of the pile by having mistakes, no matter how small, especially when there is heavy competition for the open position.

The next few pages contain several examples of details that people can miss. The following "A" examples are the examples with errors. "B" is the corrected version.

A: Incorrect
B: Correct

Below each example, I give a brief summary of the problem with the example

A: through out the day
B: throughout the day

"Throughout" is the proper way to spell throughout. Spell check won't catch this mistake because individually, "through" and "out" are spelled correctly, but used in this manner, "throughout" is the proper spelling.

A: executed on direct mail marketing campaigns
B: executed direct mail marketing campaigns

A person does not "execute on" something, they execute a plan, campaign, agenda, etc.

A: Responsible for serving costumers
B: Responsible for serving customers

The mistake here is a spelling error of "costumers" instead of "customers". "Costumers" is spelled correctly, so spell check will not pick it up – only good old proofreading will pick up this mistake.

A: cold called approximately 40 business per day
B: cold called approximately 40 businesses per day

Like the last example, "business" is spelled correctly, but if a person is calling on more than one business, it is businesses, plural.

A: Ad minister ticket sales.
B: Administer ticket sales.

Like the last two, spell check won't pick up this mistake because "ad" and "minister" are spelled correctly, but not used correctly for this example.

A: Worked in junction with
B: Worked in conjunction with

This shows a lack of language understanding. Hopefully, it was just a spelling mistake, but maybe not. As a recruiter, you aren't likely to give the person the benefit of the doubt. Nor are they going to spend much time concerned with "why", they will simply move on to the next applicant. Knowing the difference between a junction and working in conjunction with someone is important. Or a better tip would be – don't use words you aren't 100% familiar with.

A: Answered calls from prospective client
B: Answered calls from prospective clients

In this example, an "s" is missing from the end, unless there was only one prospective client. Small mistake, but noticeable.

A: Insured customer complaints were handled
B: Ensured customer complaints were handled

To insure is to arrange for compensation in the event of damage. To ensure is to make sure something is done, complete or taken care of.

And more details...

The above examples show you the mistakes that can be made in the detail of your résumé. The difference in the wording in the examples on the following pages is minor. It isn't wrong versus right. It's acceptable versus professional. It shows a higher level of skill and a higher attention to detail by using the more professional wording and/or more concise wording. The following "A" examples are generally acceptable, but the "B" example is more concise and professional.

A: ABC Company
Office Assistant
Skilled in general office duties, including answering phones, preparing correspondence, etc.

B: ABC Company
Office Assistant
Provided general administrative support, including answering phones and preparing correspondence.

A: ABC Company
Sales Intern
Called numerous lists of former/prospective clients promoting ABC company products.

B: ABC Company
Office Assistant
Made outbound calls to generate new sales leads for ABC Company.

A: ABC Company
Office Assistant
Routed calls and greeted guests.

B: ABC Company
Office Assistant
Answered incoming phone calls and greeted clients and visitors.

A: Career Objective
To obtain an internship working with the creative aspect of communication that applies the skills of production and business.

B: Career Objective
To obtain an internship in production or design.

The person here also may have been just as well off not putting in a career objective. Their background is graphic design, production, and editing. There was no need to explain what the person is looking for.

A: ABC Company
Sales Intern
Assisted in sponsorship sales along with ticket packages and promotions.

B: ABC Company
Sales Intern
Assisted in sponsorship and ticket sales. Assisted with preparation and implementation of promotions.

A: ABC Company
Customer Service Intern
Implement customer service skills by assisting clients with problems.

B: ABC Company
Customer Service Intern
Provided excellent customer service to clients by responding to and resolving problems.

A: ABC Company
Intern
Worked all the home games and two days in the office.*

B: ABC Company
Intern
Worked all home games in a variety of areas: game day promotions, sales, and marketing. Provided administrative support and assisted with pre-game preparations.

*You do not need to list how many days you worked in the office.

A: Objective:
Gain experience and utilize my skills with an internship in Finance.

B: Objective
To obtain an internship in finance that will expand upon my current knowledge and experience.

A: ABC Company
Intern
Responsible for communicating with companies to generate sales.

B: ABC Company
Intern
Sold advertising and promotions to local companies.

A: ABC Company
Objective: To obtain an internship in the sports industry with the possibility for a career.

B: ABC Company
Objective: To obtain an internship in the sports industry with the possibility for career advancement.*

*Note that if you state you are looking for career advancement and a team or company's internship program is not typically followed by a full-time position, you may not be considered for the position because you are stating that you are looking for an internship that will lead to a full-time position. You may want to have your objective statement simply state: To obtain an internship in the sports industry. This is a good example of why I don't like objective statements. You should explain in a cover letter what you are looking for. Sometimes you inadvertently taken yourself out of the running over a statement that isn't 100% accurate.

Stay away from the following wording:

- "Suggestively sold products." It just sounds *bad*. I know what you mean and so will many potential employers, but there are better ways to make your point than "suggestively sold." The proper terminology for this would be "employed suggestive selling methods to…." and explain a bit further. Example: employed suggestive selling techniques to increase initial sale to include product add-ons such as …."

- "Established/built close relationships with co-workers, executives, clients, etc." Potential employers are not looking to see how well you make friends at the office.

- "Became" in any way. "Became introduced to," "became familiar with," etc.

- "Developed … skills." I often see under responsibilities a statement that says "developed leadership skills" or "developed organizational skills". These are good statements, but better left to the cover letter. Explain what you did, not what you gained from the position. Basically, stay away from what skills you have developed or what you have learned and stick to what your responsibilities were.

- "Extensive experience" or "extremely experienced in" an area of business. At least until you've had five or more years of experience, you should not use the words "extensive" or "extremely" to describe your experience. You may have really good experience, but if you are just graduating college, the chances of you having *extensive* experience in anything yet is slim. And when you use this kind of term with someone who sees applicants who do have extensive experience in certain areas, it makes you seem unaware.

Before going on to step 4, re-read the job responsibilities that you have listed on your résumé. Do the responsibilities listed follow the advice on the previous pages? Rewrite any statements that need adjusted.

STEP 4: List any achievements or awards that were not specifically listed with a position. This is very important for students or recent college graduates who may not have much work experience.

Accomplishments – examples:
- Led department in sales.
- Received employee of the month honors.
- Dean's List
- Magna cum laude, ABC High School
- Valedictorian, ABC High School
- Honor society
- Scholarships

You can also list any major projects you did during school in this section, a thesis, a paper or a presentation you made at an academic seminar. These are excellent examples of excelling in academics. Make sure you put them on your résumé and, if appropriate, send a copy with your cover letter and résumé.

STEP 5: Fill in the rest of the résumé – activities and skills.

Activities

List any activities you have participated in – sports, clubs, volunteer work, etc. Student athletes typically learn to balance their academic and athletic commitments while in school. This is an excellent place to highlight your accomplishments on the field/court/track/ice/etc. and highlight that you were able to achieve high grades while doing so. You can also list any clubs or organizations in which you were a member or leader.

Activities – examples:
- Varsity letter winner
- Member, men's soccer team
- President, Alpha Beta Alpha
- Vice President, Student Marketing Association
- Volunteer, Red Cross

<u>Skills</u>

The skill section should highlight any special skills that weren't listed in some other section of the résumé. This is a good place for computer skills, research skills, or other skills that the employer may be looking for in a candidate.

Skills – examples:

- Able to prioritize and handle multiple projects with ease (give examples).
- Proficient with Microsoft Office (Outlook, Excel, Word, and Power Point) and Adobe
- Proficient with the use of Social Media marketing practices
- Excellent verbal and written communication skills

<u>Objective Statements</u>

I would be remiss if I did not spend a little more time on the Objective Statement. This is a newfangled trend in résumés. I will start my rant by saying emphatically and without hesitation – I HATE OBJECTIVE STATEMENTS. If you are applying for an internship or a job, as an employer, I know what your objective is. It is to obtain the internship or job you have applied for. There is no need to add this statement to a résumé. I have seen far more horrible (and I mean awful, ridiculous, poorly written and complete and utter crap) Objective Statements than I have seen good ones.

The biggest problem with Objective Statements is that it is often the first piece of content that a potential employer reads from you, the applicant. This may be your first impression if the potential employer doesn't read your cover letter. Often, with a stack of several hundred applicants, your résumé may be their first glance at your application. So, if it isn't a good statement, then you have just started off on the wrong foot. To me, there is absolutely no need for this. Also, most objective statements are focused on the applicant and not the employer. For example, a statement that reads "I am looking for a job that will be challenging and rewarding" is of little interest to the employer. You want the focus to be on why you are the best candidate, not what you are looking for in a position.

Also, if you have an objective statement that isn't broad enough then you're turning off some of the employers who are reading your résumé. You shouldn't have to tailor it to each employer and for that, you need to have a broad statement.

Again, my advice is to stay away from Objective Statements. Just leave it off the résumé. I don't know ANY employer that tosses a résumé aside for lack of an objective statement.

Now, if you *must* include a statement, please make sure that it is concise, professional and clearly refers to your knowledge, skills and abilities.

Final tip

You should save your résumé and cover letter in a format makes it look professional for online submissions. You also should save your résumé in a PDF format. Sometimes your format can get distorted if the employer uses a different version of Word. If you send in a PDF, you keep the format clean.

This also helps the employer if they save the applications for easy reference when they want to pull up your résumé again. Save your résumé in the following manner:

- Davis, Mark resume   or   Mark Davis resume
- Davis, Mark Cover Letter   or   Mark Davis Cover Letter

A variation of the above is certainly acceptable. My point is – save your résumé with a professional title.

**PROOFREAD YOUR RÉSUMÉ AT LEAST 3 TIMES.
HAVE SOMEONE ELSE PROOFREAD YOUR RÉSUMÉ.
PROOFREAD YOUR RÉSUMÉ AGAIN.**

Example: Mark Davis

Mark Davis, is a fictional job applicant. The next page is his fictional résumé. I will use him as the job applicant example throughout this book – for the résumé, cover letter and interview – so you can see the process through its entirety.

Mark Davis
123 Elm Street
Springfield, US 12345
(555) 555-5555
mdavis@email.com

Education:
University of Studies
Bachelor's Degree in Sport Management
Anticipated Graduation Date May 2013
3.7 GPA

Experience:
LMNO Company
Intern
May – August 2012
- Responsible for game day preparations, including message boards and group events
- Cold called potential customers to sell single game tickets
- Assisted with preparation and implementation of game day promotions

XYZ Company
Marketing Intern
May – August, 2011
- Organized sales lead system, including inputting and sorting information in marketing database
- Conducted market research on local college campuses regarding a new product line
- Compiled research information and presented a report to Marketing Department that highlighted market research and recommendations for college campus launch of new product line

Achievements/Awards:
- Dean's List at University of Studies, Fall 2010 – Spring 2013
- Presidential Scholarship Recipient 2012, 2013

Activities:
- Alpha Alpha Alpha Honorary Society
  - Vice President 2012-2013
  - Member 2010-2013
- Varsity Soccer Team, University of Studies
  - Captain 2012
  - Team Member 2010-2013

Skills:
- Proficient in Microsoft Office (Word, Excel, Power Point, Outlook), Internet Research, and Adobe.

-Chapter 4: Cover Letter-

*"Destiny is not a matter of chance. It is a matter of choice:
it is not to be waited for, it is a thing to be achieved."*
William Jennings Bryan

The goal of the cover letter is to get the reader to read your résumé. The reason that I go over the résumé first in this book is that the résumé provides the basis for the cover letter. Also, sometimes recruiters don't even read the cover letter unless the résumé meets certain criteria. The cover letter ties the job posting or desires of the prospective employer to your experience and skills. So, you need to have a solid résumé to start your process. Basically, this section follows the résumé writing section because you need to have already assessed your experience and skills prior to writing a cover letter.

Basics:

- ALWAYS send a cover letter. No ifs, ands or buts about this one. ALWAYS send a cover letter. Unless the posting specifically says no cover letters, send one.
- Be concise.
- Be professional.
- Address the cover letter to a person, if possible. If you are responding to a job posting, address it to the posted address.
- Focus on the employer's needs, not yours (this goes for interviewing too). Stick to why you are the best candidate for the job, not why you want the job so badly.

Beyond the Basics:

A cover letter is more than just telling the potential employer that you are passionate, experienced and hard working. You need to show that you meet the requirements by giving examples. A cover letter stating, "you should hire me because I meet all of your qualifications" does not suffice.

Tie your experience specifically to the job posting. This is the step that is most often missed by applicants. See the following tips on exactly how to do this. As a recruiter, it is refreshing and impressive when a candidate does this.

Add value at the end. The last paragraph should give the

prospective employer the sense that you not only meet their expectations, but that you have more than what they are looking for: professionalism, intelligence, maturity, etc.

Writing a Cover Letter – Step-by-Step
1. **Read the job posting.**

2. **Make a list of the qualifications and experience the employer is looking for in a candidate.**

3. **Next to the list of qualifications, write the experience you have that matches the listed item.**

4. **Draft an introductory paragraph. This paragraph should be a brief summary of what position you are applying for and a brief summary of your qualifications.**

5. **The middle paragraph or two should provide a detailed description of how your experience matches the qualifications sought for the position.**

6. **The final paragraph should summarize your education and experience and why you are a good candidate for the open position.**

Example:
1. Job posting

ABC Company has an opening for a Marketing Coordinator. The marketing coordinator is responsible for providing administrative support for the marketing department, coordination of promotional activities and maintaining marketing and ticketing databases. The ideal candidate will have a bachelor's degree in marketing, sports marketing/management, or similar area of study; excellent organizational skills; excellent verbal and written communication skills; and excellent computer skills, including experience with database software.

2. **Make a list of the qualifications and experience the employer is looking for in a candidate.**

A. Bachelor's degree in marketing, sports marketing/management or similar area of study

B. Excellent organizational skills

C. Excellent verbal and written communication skills

D. Excellent computer skills (database experience)

3. **Next to the list of qualifications, write the experience you have that matches the listed item.**

Qualification	Experience
A. Bachelor's degree in marketing, sports marketing or similar area of study	A. Bachelor's degree in sports management
B. Excellent organization skills	B. Organized office procedures to make department more efficient
C. Excellent verbal/written communication skills	C. Experience presenting promotional activities
D. Excellent computer skills including database mgmt.	D. Experience managing databases & organized sales lead databases

4. **Draft an introductory paragraph. This paragraph should be a brief summary of what position you are applying for and a brief summary of your qualifications.**

I am submitting this cover letter and résumé as my application for the Marketing Coordinator position advertised in The News newspaper.

I am a college senior and will be graduating in May of 2013, *cum laude*, with a degree in Sport Management.

5. **The middle paragraph or two should provide a detailed description of how your experience matches the qualifications sought for the position.**

I have had two internships during the past two years. The first internship was with the XYZ Company, located in Maine, whose main product line is outdoor sporting accessories. My internship was in the Marketing Department. I was responsible for organizing their sales lead system, including inputting and sorting information in their database system. I also was responsible for researching and presenting a report involving a new product line and promotional ideas for college campuses. I have included a copy of this report.

The second internship that I had was with LMNOP Company, a minor league baseball team. During this internship I was responsible for game day preparations, including message boards and group events; ticket sales and promotions. The promotions that I worked on included an in-game giveaway of T-shirts for fans who participated in a scavenger hunt and a marketing survey to gather data from guests in which there was a drawing for one person to win box seats for 10 for one game.

6. **The final paragraph should summarize your education and experience and why you are a good candidate for the open position.**

I believe that my education in sports management and internship experience have given me the organizational skills, promotional experience, and database experience that you are looking for in a Marketing Coordinator.

I am graduating in May and will be available to work full-time upon graduation. I appreciate your consideration for this position.

Pulling it all together:

The following page is a cover letter example using the above step-by-step process.

May 1, 2013

ABC Company
Attention: Human Resources
100 ABC Way
City, State 12345

Re: Application for Marketing Coordinator

Dear Hiring Manager:

I am submitting this cover letter and résumé as my application for the Marketing Coordinator position advertised in The News newspaper. I am a college senior and will be graduating in May of 2013, *cum laude*, with a degree in Sport Management.

I have had two internships during the past two years. The first internship was with the XYZ Company, located in Maine, whose main product line is outdoor sporting accessories. My internship was in the Marketing Department. I was responsible for organizing their sales lead system, including inputting and sorting information in their database system. I also was responsible for researching and presenting a report involving a new product line and promotional ideas for college campuses. I have included a copy of this report.

The second internship that I had was with LMNOP Company, a minor league baseball team. During this internship I was responsible for game day preparations, including message boards and group events; ticket sales and promotions. The promotions that I worked on included an in-game giveaway of T-shirts for fans who participated in a scavenger hunt and a marketing survey to gather data from guests in which there was a drawing for one person to win box seats for 10 for one game.

I believe that my education in sports management and internship experience have given me the organizational skills, promotional experience, and database experience that you are looking for in a Marketing Coordinator.

I am graduating in May and will be available to work full-time upon graduation. I appreciate your consideration for this position.

Sincerely,

Mark Davis

PROOFREAD RÉSUMÉ AND COVER LETTER THREE TIMES BEFORE SENDING!

-Chapter 5: Application Process-

"If we are growing, we are always
going to be outside our comfort zone"
John C. Maxwell

Before starting any application process, you should ask yourself
these questions:

What do I want from a job? (ex. money, prestige, experience,
job satisfaction, company location)

What do I want from an employer? (ex. money, experience,
career path, mentoring, job security)

What kind of work environment do I want? (ex. cubicle,
office, travel, field work, interaction with people)

What type of company do you want to work for? (ex.
college athletics, professional sports, sports apparel,
agency, etc.)

How much money do you need to live? (ex. rent/house
payment, car payment, bills, loans, fun money)

Once you have an idea of what you need out of a job, then you can
start being more discerning about the types of positions that you apply
for. If you need to make a certain base salary, then you need to apply
for jobs that fall into that range. If you have in mind what you want for
your career path, then you need to choose jobs that fall within your
desired path. If location (geographically) is important to you, then you
will want to apply for jobs in that specific area. (Tip: The more you
limit your geographic location, the more you limit the opportunities in
sports. Geographic mobility equals more opportunities in sports.)

You will see that most of the advice in this book deals with applying
for a job opening. That is because your best chance at landing a job is
for a position that is open. However, I thought it would be helpful to
give you some tips in some of the different types of application
situations: mass marketing yourself, pre-applying for jobs that aren't
available yet, career fair applications and applying for a posted position.

Mass Marketing Yourself

First, let's cover mass marketing yourself or in other words, sending out hundreds of résumés to companies that aren't necessarily hiring. The typical process is this: you make 100 copies of your résumé; generate 100 generic cover letters with a mail merge program that lets you put different addressees on the letter and you mail these directly to the companies. While this isn't the most effective manner of applying for jobs, it is a typical process and does have a small chance for success, depending on the company, team or program with whom you are applying.

Do not solely rely on the mass marketing method. It brings you the least chance for success.

Pre-applying for a job

Pre-applying for a job can be a good way to get in front of potential hiring managers. From informational interviews to internships – this is what you're doing. Pre-applying for a job.

Informational Interviews are interviews that you request from a Human Resources representative or manager in a department in which you are interested in working. You've made a connection somehow (see Chapter 6 on Networking for connection ideas) and you are in front of someone who may not have an immediate opening, but you are there to ask him or her about their career, their department, their company and any future openings. This is a great way to get introduced to a company and make a good impression.

If you have an internship, you should view it as an in-person pre-application situation. In other words, treat your internship like an extended job interview. More than likely, your employer is treating it this way. You should too. Get to know people in your department and throughout the company. Get involved. Volunteer for extra events. Make a good impression. Work hard. Work smart. Be a go-to person. This way, when and if an open position arises, you have numerous people in the organization who are able to vouch for you as to why you should be considered for the job.

Career Fairs

Career Fairs are another way to get in front of hiring managers. Sometimes career fairs will get you in front of someone who has an immediate opening, so this may be a true job application, but sometimes employers at a career fair are recruiting ahead, or seeing who is out there for future openings. Either way, this is a great way to make a good impression on someone.

I remember a young woman I met at a career fair. She was a junior in college at the time, but just wanted to introduce herself and find out what type of career openings we typically had for college graduates. She said that she wasn't graduating for another year, but was trying to find out ahead of time what she should do over the next year to increase her chances of a job upon graduation. She came across as intelligent, friendly, positive and proactive. I kept in touch with her over that year and we hired her upon graduation the following year. Her enthusiasm, energy and forward thinking were exactly the type of traits we were looking for.

Career fairs in sports are different from career fairs in other industries. The set up is often similar. There are a number of employers spending a short amount of time with job applicants at a booth or table to determine whether or not they might consider the applicant for an internship or job. However, at a typical career fair, a student can visit several different potential employers and hand them their résumé and the employer will do a lot of the talking. The employer often brings a nice tablecloth and some kind of visual aid/prop that outlines why candidates should consider working for the company. They bring all kinds of "goodies" to take with you. I've seen Chap Stick, Band-Aids, pens, pads of paper, key chains and other items that you can take away and remember what a great employer they might be.

That is not how it typically works at a career fair for sports. You might see a potential employer with a nice set up, but most sports teams and/or universities will expect you to have some knowledge of who they are. They are fortunate that don't have to spend a lot of time explaining who they are, what their product is or why their company is so great to work for. Some teams/schools will spend a little bit of time on this, but not much. They expect you to have some basic knowledge about their company. What they might spend some time explaining are the types of opportunities they have, what departments might have openings or how their sales program is set up and how they hire into that program. But it isn't about selling you on their opportunities. It's about you selling yourself to them about what a great candidate you are.

Your best results will be if you walk up to a potential employer, hand them your résumé and look them in the eye and give them a short statement about your name, education and background. Look them in the eye. Be positive. Be confident.

Here is an example:

"Hi. My name is Mark. Here is a copy of my résumé. I'm a student at University of Studies. My major is Sport Management and I'm looking for a full-time position. I have had two internships where I gained a variety of experience. I am most interested in positions in marketing or sales, but am open to a variety of positions, as I think my experience has prepared me for a variety of positions with your company. Can you tell me about any opportunities you have available?"

Chapter 9 gives you advice about your 30-second elevator speech or what I prefer to call your brand statement. Opening with your brand statement is a great way to introduce yourself.

If this kind of communication isn't something you're comfortable with, then my best advice is to get out of your comfort zone. Understand that this is the time to sell yourself and your abilities and you might need to step out of a comfortable place to make a good impression.

Applying for a posted position

Applying for a posted position is by far the most likely scenario that will lead you to a job. A job is posted, you send in an application (cover letter, résumé, supporting materials) and you wait for a response from Human Resources, a recruiter or a hiring manager.

You want to make sure that you are applying for jobs that match your education and experience. With online job applications now, a recruiter can often tell if you've applied for multiple positions. Applying for multiple positions is acceptable, as long as those jobs are similar or you are similarly qualified. If you apply for Inside Sales and Senior Marketing Manager in the same six-month time span, it shows the recruiter that you don't know your skill set and it reeks of desperation. Inside sales is an entry-level position. Senior Marketing Manager generally requires at least 5 years of experience. Rarely would the same person qualify for both. One is entry level. The other requires 5 years of experience. If you are applying for positions that don't have the same requirements, then it makes you look like you're not serious and that you don't understand the employer as a business, but only as sports entity.

Keep in mind that the recruiter isn't going to be looking for someone who just wants to work in sports. They want someone who wants to do the job that they would be hired to do. Now, if you apply in a short amount of time for Inside Sales, Marketing Coordinator, and Public Relations Assistant or the like, you're probably OK because those are positions that have similar education and experience requirements.

Your best bet with job applications, though, is to use your network. Find someone in your network that knows someone. It significantly increases your chances of having your résumé reviewed for the position and the possibility of interview. And focuses on the jobs that match your education and experience.

It is possible to get a job in sports without a network. For those without a solid network, I advise you to volunteer, get advanced education, lead clubs and/or association, participate, be involved, get experience, and do whatever you can to make yourself stand out and focus on education and experience that is going to bring value to a company.

<u>Applying online</u>

With the increasing use of online applications, it is important to know and understand how this technology works. There are a few different ways that online application technology works.

First, there is applicant-tracking software that will do the applicant screening for some employers. Therefore, the first review of your résumé may not be a person, but a computer. For these kinds of systems, you will need to have certain key words or buzz words in your résumé or application. Those words change based on the type of position, so I can't give you exact advice on what needs to be in your résumé. However, it is extremely important to be honest and concise in your descriptions of your positions and jobs and your best bet is to look at the job posting to see if your résumé uses the same type of wording to describe your experience. For example, if a company is looking for database marketing experience, make sure your resume has the words "database marketing" specifically in your résumé. I know this contradicts the "don't tailor your résumé" advice I've given you, but as technology changes, so do we. It might be a valid time to tweak your résumé depending on the words used in the job posting.

Second, some online systems do not have an initial computer review of résumés and works simply as an easier, more convenient tool for organizing, reviewing and responding to applicants. So, the first review of your résumé may still be a person, even if you apply online.

For either type of online applicant system, you will often see a variety of questions posed to you as you either enter information into the system or after you post your résumé. My best advice for these kinds of questions is to be honest. I cannot stress this enough. If you are applying for a job that asks whether you have a minimum of two years of sales experience and you don't have that experience, do not mark "yes" thinking that will get you further in the process. Usually the questions posed are to help narrow down the applicant pool. And yes, you may have to answer questions that don't match what the employer wants. This should lead you to a couple of obvious thoughts: (1) maybe you aren't the right fit for this job or (2) maybe the employer has hundreds of applicants and needs to find some way to get the applicant pool more manageable for review and that maybe you might not make the cut or (3) maybe your answer won't affect your status negatively, but the employer is grouping applicants by experience for review and not necessarily using it to weed people out. I could go on and on about the possibilities of how employers use these questions. The important thing is that you are honest. If you lie here and then get to the interview process by saying you have experience that you do not, you've wasted your time and their time and that's not a good way to make a good impression on a potential employer.

Where are the jobs?

There are a variety of resources for you. If you are still in school or a recent graduate, your school's career services office is a great place to start for guidance and job postings. But don't just rely on one source. You really have to be your own job advocate. Visit career services. Talk to your professors. Attend career fairs. And today, technology is incredible. You can follow job postings from a variety of companies easily and quickly on your smart phone, iPad or tablet, or computer. @Teamworkonline posts new jobs on Twitter with a link to the actual job posting. All you have to do is follow @Teamworkonline and a job posting will be sent to you. There is so much out there for you – use it.

Following is a small sample to get you started in what tools are available to you on the Internet. This is just to get you started. There are several other companies and websites that are available with excellent job postings and career advice.

General Job/Career Websites:

www.monster.com
www.careerbuilder.com
www.simplyhired.com
www.indeed.com (this is a site that pulls postings from other sites. Employers don't actually post on indeed.com so watch out to make sure that postings are up to date. Otherwise, it is a great site).

Job/Career Websites, specific to the Sport Industry:

www.teamworkonline.com
www.workinsports.com
www.jobsinsports.com
www.womensportsjobs.com
www.espncareers.com
www.sportsearchonline.com
www.thesportsresume.com

Website with information on getting a degree (undergraduate and/or graduate) in Sport Management/Sport Administration:

www.degreesinsports.com

Also, there are some great resources to follow on Twitter:

@workinsports
@teamworkonline
@jobsinsports
@breakintosports
@sportsjobfinder
@socialhire.com
@dreamcareersinc
@elitecareers1
@sportscareers
@espncareers
@simplyhired

@TheSportsResume
@sportsearch
@careerbuilder

Most of the above Twitter accounts are specific to those looking for jobs in sports, but there are also a couple of resources out there that aren't specific to sports, but have a great amount of knowledge and advice for college students as they transition into their careers. My favorites are:

@hrlegalconsult (that's my Twitter account)
@lindsaypollak
@greatonthejob

Teams, leagues, conferences, and other sport related entities have their own websites, such as:

www.nfl.com
www.nba.com
www.mlb.com
www.nhl.com
www.mls.com
www.nascar.com
www.ncaa.com
www.bigten.org
www.mac-sports.com
www.themwc.com
www.secdigitalnetwork.com

AND so on… As easy as the Internet is to use, find a search engine, type in the name of the team and there you have it. Many companies have a link at the very bottom of their webpage for Employment, under front office, or contact information. Many team websites and college websites will either direct you to their internal recruiting web page or to a webpage of a company that handles their job postings for them. You just have to look.

-Chapter 6: Networking-

"It's not what you know. It's who you know"
-Unknown

For many, networking is an unfamiliar or scary concept. Many students or job applicants don't understand how to use the people they know to increase their chances of an interview. Most research shows that only a fraction of people intuitively know how to network.[1]

So, I will start at the beginning for networking. Basically, a network is a group of personal and professional contacts. Networking is the deliberate process of exchanging information, resources, support and access in such a way as to create a mutually beneficial relationship for personal and professional success.[2] Most people shy away from networking because they think that it means they have to be extremely outgoing or they have to go do something to make this happen. Basically, good networking should be happening all the time. Making good connections with people you know – teachers, co-workers, classmates, supervisors, subordinates, interns, etc.

To keep it simple, ask yourself some questions about who you know.

Start with family, friends and neighbors. Then...

Who do you know from school? (Current and previous)
What teachers do you know?
What people have you served on committees or in clubs with?
Who was on your athletic team?
Who have you worked with in internships?
Who are members of service or professional organizations?
Who has been your supervisor?
Who have you supervised?
Who have you been in class with?
Who have you worked on a project with?
Who do you know well enough to advocate on your behalf for a job or internship?

---

[1] Anne Baber and Lynne Waymon. *Make Your Contacts Count, 2nd Edition*. (New York: American Management Association, 2007), 17.
[2] Ibid.

Ah… technology. It truly is magical. LinkedIn, Google+, and other professional networking sites are a tremendous asset to you. You should use them regularly. These sites make it VERY easy to create, track and communicate with your network on a regular basis. You will even get prompts of people you may know. Technology is cheap and effective. Use it.

Events are a good way to add connections to your network. If you're not naturally outgoing, then I suggest, again, that you learn to get out of your comfort zone. Not everyone is naturally outgoing and wants to interact with other people at networking events, but sometimes it takes getting out of your comfort zone to get to know people who may help you in your career.

Networking Tips

There are a few keys to expanding your network successfully. You can have 500+ connections via LinkedIn, but if they don't know you and can't vouch for you, then you haven't really built a true network. You just have a bunch of people who see what you post on LinkedIn.

Tip 1: Be recommendable: As with everything, start with yourself. The people who find it easy to build a network aren't necessarily those that are the most outgoing, but those that connect with others. You have to first be the kind of person another person would recommend or the kind of person another person is willing to connect with a hiring manager. And you do that every day. You've probably heard the mantra "always be interviewing". Well, you should also "always be networking". If you make genuine connections with people and are the kind of person (trustworthy, hard worker, mature, professional, etc.) that others are willing to attach their name to − that's how you become recommendable.

Tip 2: Reach out to your network. It's an accepted practice to reach out to your network and ask for help. It's also acceptable to reach out to people that you might know in a marginal way if you have decent connections between you. But as you reach out, you must be professional. Don't just ask for the favor of a recommendation or introduction to a hiring professional. Make a connection first. Show them who you are and why they should take the time to help you out. Be professional. Following are some examples.

Example A:

Dear Professor:

I hear you used to work for a hockey team. I love hockey and really want to work for a hockey team. I am a friend of Bob Smith, who is a student in your class. I have attached my résumé. Please forward this to anyone you know in hockey. I really appreciate your help.

Thanks,
Mark Adams

This example is wrong on so many levels, but it is a sample of what I've seen and is similar to what other professionals receive. I have no real connection to the person, I don't know anything about their qualifications or work ethic, and I don't know why I should take the time to extend my business reputation for this person.

You need to make a real connection with your network, not just use it as a forwarding service for jobs.

Example B:

Dear Professor:

My name is Mark Adams. I am a good friend and ex-teammate of Bob Smith, a student in your class. I am a senior in College at XYZ University and will be graduating cum laude with a double major in Business and Sport Management. I've had two internships with sports teams doing a variety of jobs from ticket sales to game operations. I've worked really hard to maintain a high GPA and have gained some valuable experience from the internships I've had.

I understand that you used to work for a professional sports team and Bob said you have been able to help him as he applies for jobs in the sports industry. I have attached my résumé and would appreciate any feedback you might be able to give me as I apply for a job in the sport industry.

Thank you so much for your time.

Sincerely,

Mark Adams

Two key elements in the second example are: professional tone and content. It is written in a business-like manner and gives the reader some idea of why they should care (friend of someone they know) and that they are qualified for the positions they are seeking (GPA, experience). It doesn't assume the reader is going to jump at the chance of helping him out. It simply asks for some advice.

Example C: (A good example for when you are reaching out to someone you don't know or someone you marginally know)

Dear Mr. Mister:

My name is Mark Adams and I am a senior in College at XYZ University and will be graduating with a degree in Sport Management in May. I've had two internships with minor league sports teams, doing a variety of jobs from ticket sales to game operations. I've worked really hard to prepare my self for a career in the sport industry, but would be grateful for some advice from someone who has made a successful career in sports.

I really appreciate you taking the time to read this email and I am hopeful that you might be able to find a few minutes in the coming weeks for a quick call where I could ask you for some advice on where I'm headed after graduation. I'm glad to make whatever time work, if you just let me know what you might have available. I'll be glad to give you a call.

Thank you,

Mark Adams

One way to increase your chances at an interview is to use your network. Keep in mind that a person who applies for a job and has a network connection to the company, human resources department or hiring manager has a much better shot at getting an interview than someone whose résumé is sitting in a stack (or virtual stack) of résumés. The best way to explain it is as follows. A recruiter or hiring manager typically has two piles of résumés, referred résumés and unknown applicants. If the referred résumé stack has 10 résumés in it, that stack will likely stay at 10 or close to that as the hiring manager goes through the applicant review process. However, the unknown pile that is maybe 100 résumés will be whittled down to 10-25, depending on the position. When a hiring manager hears from someone that they know and respect that an applicant is worth looking at, the hiring manager usually looks at them.

In Sports, more than any other industry, networking is key. In sports, people move from company to company or team to team on a regular basis, and it isn't frowned upon, generally. It's fairly standard. It's the odd situation that a person is with an organization for a lengthy period of time. "Why?" you ask. Well, in order to move up in sports, you often have to move out. Many teams, athletic departments, leagues and conferences have small departments and therefore when a person has been in a certain role for a certain period of time, they need to look out in order to move up. It's just the nature of the business and the structure of the team or athletic department. If a person wants to be an Athletic Director, they might take the path like this: Event Coordinator for ABC University Athletic Department (3 years), Ticket Office Manager XYZ University Athletic Department (2 years), Assistant Athletic Director at LMNO University Athletic Department (5 years) and Athletic Director DEF University Athletic Department. This is a pretty typical path. So, that person who has over ten years of experience will know people at four different universities and has several connections at each.

As I stated in the previous chapter, you have a much higher chance of landing an interview if someone knows someone who can vouch for you. Use your network contacts. It isn't a foreign practice; people do it all the time. Employers expect it and often welcome it. I know that I had a go-to executive for referrals. If he sent someone to us for an open position, I knew that the applicant would be professional, mature and would be well worth our time. I loved to get referrals from the executive because I knew it meant a solid candidate for the job. Good referrals make the recruiting process a lot easier on the hiring committee. When people have so many other responsibilities and things to do, that is a welcome thing. Your goal should be to be the one being referred by the well-respected executive or manager who can help make a difference in your application process.

So, we started this chapter with the quote: "it's not what you know but who you know." **In sports, it's what you know AND who you know**. You have to have basic education, experience and skills and be the right fit for the job. And it helps to have a great network.

-Chapter 7: References-

"Nothing will work unless you do."
-John Wooden

References can be included with the initial résumé, but it isn't necessary to include on the initial application. Certainly, do not include references on the résumé. References should be a separate attachment or page in your application packet. There was a trend for a while to include a statement that says "references available upon request". I think this statement works fine for a person who is currently employed that wants to maintain confidentiality until they are a *bona fide* candidate for a job. However, if you are a college student or recent college graduate, you can include a list of two to three references with every application. This is a good indication to the potential employer that you have professors and/or employers who are willing to vouch for your work ethic and/or ability to do a good job.

References should be someone who can actually speak to your ability. It should be someone who directly supervised your work and can attest to more than just that you are a good person. Coaches, professors, supervisors at previous internships are all good references.

It does help if you can get someone at a high level from a company to serve as a reference. A CEO, President, Athletic Director, Vice President, or department head is a good person to have as a reference. It shows that you were involved in high-level activities at your job or internship to interact with a high level employee who knows enough about you to serve as a reference.

It should go without saying, but don't forget to contact your references ahead of time to make sure that they are agreeable to being listed as a reference. It is also helpful if you give your references an updated copy of your résumé so they can use it to be more specific in their recommendation.

When listing references, list the name, title, company, address and phone number of the reference. You should also list your relationship with the reference. For example, if you list a VP of ABC Company, you should state that they were the head of the department you interned with and whether they were your direct supervisor.

If you do include references, then references should be listed on a second/separate page. If you list references at the bottom of the page, keep the information simple: Name, Company, Title, telephone number and their relationship to you.

EXAMPLE:

Mary Smith
Vice President of Marketing
ABC Company
(555) 555-5555
I worked with this reference during my internship with ABC Company.

Robert Lee
Marketing Manager
ABC Company
(555) 555-5555
This reference served as my direct supervisor during my internship with ABC Company.

It also can be helpful to send a copy of a letter of recommendation with your cover letter and résumé. Now, some electronic application processes will not allow for extra attachments, but if you can, adding a copy of a letter of recommendation won't hurt your chances. Especially in sports. Many people are connected, even if they work in different sports or different areas. Sports is such a transient business that people have connections everywhere. USE THEM!

-Chapter 8: Interviewing-

"You may have to fight a battle more than once to win it."
Margaret Thatcher

So, you've made it to the interview. You've successfully opened the door. Now it is your time to shine. Your job now is one thing – to sell yourself. In a very professional and confident manner, you need to explain what you bring to the table for this position and why you are the best candidate for the job.

Basically, an interview is a communication exchange between a potential employer (one, two or more interviewers) and a job applicant. The purpose of this exchange is for the employer to assess whether the applicant has the knowledge, skills and ability to perform the job. The employer is also looking for behavior indicators that will help predict the success of the applicant. In other words, the employer is trying to see whether there are indications from the interview that will predict whether the person can do the job and will be a good employee.

Interviews are a two way street. Don't forget that the applicant is trying to determine whether the job, department, supervisor and company are the right first (or next) step in their career.

Employers know that good employees make a positive impact on the success of a company, so they employ a variety of techniques to predict whether the candidate will fulfill their needs and expectations for the position. They may use a prescreening or phone interview. They may do interviews at job/career fairs. They may use prescreening questionnaires that are sent to candidates prior to selecting interview candidates. They most likely will have some face-to-face interview process. And they may use some kind of pre-employment testing that can range from drug testing to personality tests (Jung Typology Test TM, Myers-Briggs Type Indicator, Caliper, Predictive Index, Wonderlic Personnel Test) to specific ability tests (accounting, computer programming, typing, computer software use, etc.).

Prescreening and/or Phone Interviews

Candidates often underestimate the importance of a prescreening or phone interview. Employers use various styles for prescreening, but it is often used when an employer has narrowed the field, but is unable to bring in all the candidates for an interview and wants to narrow the field even further. So, a prescreening questionnaire that is emailed or a prescreening phone interview is used to narrow down the applicants to candidates the employer is willing to bring in for interview.

The key here is that this is a significant part of the process and should be taken seriously. Prepare as you would for a typical interview situation. Find time and space where you can talk privately without interruption. If you are completing a questionnaire, set aside time to really review the questions and answers that you are providing. If you're doing Skype – look at the camera, not the screen. Basically, treat it as seriously as you would an in-person interview. So, the following information and advice should apply to prescreening just as much as a face-to-face interview situation.

Interviews

Employers have various interview styles. Often an interviewer will use more than one style of interviewing. If you interview with more than one person from a company, more than likely you'll see several different styles and combinations of interviewing and testing before you are selected for a position.

Traditional interviewing is the type of interviewing that asks basic questions to the interviewee. Examples of traditional interviewing questions:

- How would you describe yourself?
- What are your short term career goals?
- What are your long term career goals?
- Why do you want to work in sports?
- What are your strengths?
- What are your weaknesses?
- Why did you leave your current position?
- What aspect of your previous position did you like the best?
- What aspect of your previous position did you like the least?
- What motivates you to put forth your greatest effort?
- Which subjects in college were you most successful?
- Which subjects in college did you struggle with?
- Which aspects of your education did you enjoy the most and why?
- If I were to talk with your references, what would they say about you?

With traditional interview questions, the employer is looking for the actual answer to the question, but also interviewers are looking for how the interviewee answers. Do they give short concise answers? Do they go on and on? Do they provide coherent, intelligent answers or do they offer rambling answers that don't make much sense. Are they able to answer in a professional manner? Did they actually answer the question that was asked or did they find a way to present a prepared answer or statement?

Be prepared to discuss your major and the classes you have taken in college. Be prepared to answer questions such as:

· Why did you choose MAJOR (finance, communications, sport management, etc.) as a major?
· What does MAJOR (strategic communications, business, accounting, etc.) prepare you for as a career?
· What kind of classes did you take that might be relevant to the position you are applying for?
· What extracurricular activities did you participate in that might be relevant to the position?

Behavioral interviewing is the type of interviewing that tries to understand the behavior of the applicant by asking questions about how they handled certain situations in the past. Employers are typically looking for detail in these questions, so make sure to be specific in your answers. Examples of behavioral interview questions:

· Give me an example of a time when you had several tasks to do and you had to prioritize your tasks.
· Give me an example of a goal you set for yourself and tell me what you did to reach that goal.
· Describe a time when you were faced with a stressful situation that demonstrated your coping skills.
· Give me an example of when you were asked to go above and beyond normal expectations to complete a job or achieve a goal.

There are several other types of interview styles that you may see, but I believe the best way to prepare for an interview is to focus on yourself and not prepare answers for questions that may never be asked.

Preparing for Your Interview

There are a lot of different opinions on preparing for a job interview. You can read books and prepare for the different questions that might be asked of you. As listed above, there are several basic questions that you can prepare to answer. However, my best advice to you is to focus on yourself, not what you think the interviewer might ask. Now, don't confuse this with the advice that I give that you have to keep your cover letter and interviews focused on the employer needs. You still need to do that. And you do need to research the company. *But in the preparation stage, you want to focus on yourself and focus on how you bring value to the company.* There are far too many possibilities of questions and interview styles to prepare appropriately. If you focus on yourself, reviewing your qualifications, working on your presentation of yourself (be confident, maintain eye contact, etc.), you'll be more efficient in the use of your time and more prepared for any and all interviews that you may face.

Also, you never know whether someone is going to toss your résumé aside, like Molly Fletcher describes in *Your Dream Job Game Plan*[3]. When Molly went to meet with a Sport Marketing company, they tossed her résumé aside and asked "Molly, who are you? And what do you want to do?" If you've successfully prepared for the interview, you are ready for these questions. Even if the résumé is in the trash, you should be able to talk about it as a conversation, rather than a list of items from a piece of paper.

Interview – The Basics
- Be 10-15 minutes early
- Dress professionally (A business suit is a good start. Even if the interviewer is in business casual, likely they may not be dressed like that on a daily basis).
- Be confident
- Be consistent. (If you say you are energetic and a go-getter – act like it. If you say you are excited to be there – smile and look like it)
- Be positive. Even if you have had some negative experiences with past employers, teachers, coaches, etc. Stay away from the negativity.
- Have a good solid handshake. Not overpowering, but firm – one that shows confidence.
- Listen. Listen. Listen. Often in sports, applicants are so excited to be interviewing for a job in sports that they lose sight of the importance of asking questions and understanding the position that they are interviewing for. Be discerning. Ask questions. Don't just take any job, just because it is in sports. Make sure the job is the

---

[3] Fletcher, Molly. *Your Dream Job Game Plan. 5 Tools for Becoming Your Own Career Agent.* (Indianapolis, IN: JIST Works, 2009), 9.

right fit for you too. I always hated hearing from people in an exit interview that yes, they were told what the job was, but they didn't really care because they just wanted a job in sports, only to find out two months later that they didn't really enjoy doing the job they were hired to do. You're better for yourself (and selfishly, I'd argue for the employer) if you listen and make sure that you want to do the job you are hired to do, not just work in sports.

- If you are a man planning on wearing a suit and tie (probably a good idea), make sure you know how to tie a tie. It sounds obvious, but scrambling before the interview and tying a tie that looks sloppy really does make an impression on the interviewers, and not a good one.

- Research the company ahead of time. At least know the basics. There is so much information available via the Internet – use it. Know the basics of the team, university, conference, league, facility, etc. that you are visiting. Know what's going on in the news in that area that relates to the team, university or facility. Read the local news online. Do a search of the company, department and people you are meeting with. Look them up on LinkedIn and review their profiles. And know some brief history about the team, university or facility. Know if they are facing any hardships (labor disputes, NCAA sanctions, etc.) and/or if they have any businesses deals that have made the news. The Internet, *Sports Business Journal,* and other sport-related publications can provide you with information that will be helpful in the interview. I remember interviewing an applicant at a career fair in the spring of 2005. He didn't even know there was an NHL lockout going on. That is certainly not going to get you to the next step in the hiring process.

- Be yourself. You are trying to find the right fit for your career as much as they are trying to find the right job candidate. Or at least you should be. If you try to be someone you are not, it will be apparent within a few weeks of your new job that this isn't going to be a good fit. Also, know that you may have very similar interviews with two different people, but they will come away with different impressions. One interviewer may find you engaging and delightful and another may find you too talkative. You just don't know what the interviewer's perspective is, so your best bet is to be yourself to find that right fit for both you and the employer.

Beyond the Basics

I highly recommend you stay away from the following phrases: "I just want to get my foot in the door," "I understand that I might have to start in ticketing," and "I don't care what I do, I just want to work in sports."

"I just want to get my foot in the door." This signals to the person interviewing you that you're more concerned with being able to tell people that you work for a sports team than actually doing the job that you might be hired to do. This is not a good place to start in the interview process. There are plenty of candidates who know what they have to offer and are able to express that to hiring managers. You may really just want to get your foot in the door and that's fine, just don't be so blunt and say it in your interview.

"I understand that I might have to start in ticketing." To a ticketing professional this can be an extremely offensive statement. You're basically saying to him/her that you're much better than having to work in ticketing, but you'll start there if you have to. Also, by saying that people will "have to" start in ticketing somehow implies that it isn't a good job or isn't a good place to start. In some sports, ticketing is the main revenue source and therefore a crucial part of the team's business operations. "Having to" start in a crucial part of the business isn't a bad deal. Also, ticketing can provide you with skills that you may not have yet attained. It can be relevant and helpful job experience that leads you to your next position. It shouldn't only be thought of as the place where you "have to start." And getting good sales experience anywhere will be valuable to your career.

"I don't care what I do. I just want to work in sports." Or "I don't care what I do. I just want to work for (INSERT TEAM/COLLEGE NAME HERE)." These phrases will easily get you to the bottom of the list. If you don't know yourself well enough to explain not only what area you are most interested in, but what area your skills are the best fit for, you will easily lose out to the competition who is prepared to explain why they would be an asset as an employee and not just why it would be so great to work for the team.

Job and career fairs are basically a mini-interview and are a great place to make a first impression. This is where you can showcase your positive attitude, enthusiasm, passion and intelligence without having to rely on the cover letter and résumé getting your foot in the door. You're in the door at career fairs. It's just a matter of what you do with it.

Make sure you are able to give detailed examples of what is listed on your résumé. Make sure that you can explain your job/intern experience. If you have listed "excellent organization skills" under "Skills" make sure that you can give a detailed example of how you know you have excellent organizational skills. If you listed "trustworthy employee" explain that you were given the responsibility of opening, closing and handling night deposits with your previous employer.

Interview Outline

I highly recommend creating an Interview Outline. This outline prepares you for several questions and reviews your history. Obviously, you know what you've done and should be able to answer questions about yourself without much preparation. However, in order to recall the information in a way that you can quickly present in a professional manner, I recommend treating an interview like a public speaking assignment. Have an outline prepared in your head with speaking points and basic information.

I. Educational History
   A. Undergraduate education
      1. Major:
         a. Classes taken, short description and how class might relate to position interviewing for
      2. Minor:
         a. Classes taken, short description and how class might relate to position interviewing for
      3. Why I chose this area of study
      4. What types of positions this area of study prepared me for
   B. Graduate education
      1. Focus of study (MBA, MSA, J.D., PhD)
         a. Classes taken, short description and how class might relate to position interviewing for
      2. Why I chose this area of study
      3. What types of positions this area of study prepared me for
      4. What thesis or research work I did during my graduate studies.
      5. Special projects completed
II. RÉSUMÉ (Have a copy with you)
   A. Work History (including internships)
      1. Position with Company
         a. Responsibilities
         b. Responsibilities
         c. Achievements
         d. How this experience is relevant/beneficial to position interviewing for
   B. Activities
   C. Awards/Distinctions
III. Career Goals
   A. Short Term
   B. Long Term
IV. Summary statement of why you are the best candidate for the job

There is a difference between preparing for an interview and preparing answers for an interview. I recommend preparing for an interview. I do not recommend preparing answers. However, most employers either offer up a final question of "Is there anything we haven't covered today that you would like us to know" or "In two minutes or less, please summarize for me why you are the best candidate for the job" or something similar. This is something that you should be prepared for. Chapter 9 has more detailed advice about developing a brand statement.

Below is an example of an Interview Outline for the fictional Mark Davis:

Interview Outline – Mark Davis

I. Educational History
    A. Undergraduate education: University of Studies
        1. Major: Sport Management
            a. Introduction to Sport Management: overview of business of sports – college athletics, professional sports, amateur sports, Olympics.
            b. Sport Marketing: overview of how marketing in sports is different from marketing traditional products. Sports are perishable, intangible and unpredictable. Plus competing and cooperation is very different in sports.
            c. Communication: basic public speaking class. Practiced presenting ideas in a clear, logical manner.
        2. Minor: Business
            a. Business Management: overview of general business practices.
            b. Accounting: general accounting procedures – debits/credits,
        3. Why I chose this area of study
            a. I chose to major in Sport Management because I wanted to be prepared for a career in sports. I have always had an interest in sports from a competitive standpoint and wanted to learn about the business side of the sport industry to become more familiar with sport industry business practices and to gain insights into the types of careers that are found in the sport industry.
        4. What types of positions this area of study prepared me for
            a. Marketing, Sales, Public Relations, Customer Service
    B. Graduate education
        1. No graduate education yet. Plan to work for a few years

then pursue either a Masters of Sports Administration or Masters of Business Administration Degree.

II. RÉSUMÉ
   A. Work History
      1. Internship – LMNO Company
         a. Responsible for game day preparations, including message boards and group events
         b. Cold called potential customers to sell single game tickets
         c. Assisted with preparation and implementation of game day promotions
         d. This experience is relevant because it has given me experience in working in sports – seeing the ins and outs of several departments, from promotions to ticketing to game day operations.
      2. Internship – XYZ Company
         a. Organized sales lead system, including inputting and sorting information in Marketing database
         b. Conducted market research on local college campuses regarding a new product line
         c. Compiled research information and presented a report to Marketing Department that highlighted market research and recommendations for college campus launch of new product line
         d. This experience is relevant because it gave me experience working with a marketing database and seeing the significance of using a customer relations management system and the hands on experience of doing market research on a college campus. I was able to see the product line development, market research and the development of a marketing plan for the launch of a new product line.
   B. Activities
      1. While I was in school, I was a member of the Soccer Team. We were Division Champions my sophomore year, which was a tremendous experience from a competition standpoint. We just missed the finals in my senior year, when I was the Captain of the team.
      2. I learned a lot from being a student athlete. I learned to manage my time well. I learned to balance and manage

priorities to ensure that I met both my commitment to myself academically and to my team.

C.   Awards/Distinctions

    1. I was named to the Dean's List every semester while at University of Studies.

    2. I received the Presidential Scholarship for my Junior and Senior years.

III. Career Goals

A.   Short Term

    1. To obtain a position in Marketing for a Professional Sports Team.

B.   Long Term

    1. To obtain a Masters Degree, after 2-4 years of working in the Sport Industry.

    2. To become a leader and successful marketer in the Sport Industry.

IV. Summary statement of why you are the best candidate for the job

A.   I am the best candidate for the Marketing Coordinator position because I have the education and experience to do a good job for your company. I have had two internships that have prepared me for an entry-level position. I was able to maintain a high GPA while also being a student athlete in college. And above all, I have a positive attitude and a good work ethic to be an excellent employee for your company.

<u>Asking questions in an interview</u>

Don't ask questions just for the sake of asking them. It may be difficult for an inexperienced candidate to ask too many questions. Employers know this and usually have reasonable expectations. However, a good interview question shows knowledge of the industry, company or position and relates to those areas.[4] Stay away from questions about time off or benefits, as those are personal issues and not related to the position. Leave those for when and if a job offer is made. The initial interview questions should focus on the company or position.

At the end of the interview, you should have enough information to

---

[4] Eric P. Kramer, *Active Interviewing, Branding, Selling and Presenting Yourself to Win Your Next Job*, (Boston: Cengage Technology, 2012), 125.

make a decision of whether or not to accept the position, if it is offered. You should understand, in general, the duties and responsibilities of the position you would be accepting, who your supervisor would be, and what your role in the department and/or company would be. If you don't have enough information, then the question to yourself is – what else do you need to know to make an informed decision about accepting the position? Then ask the interviewer those questions.

If you really struggle with what to ask, here are a few good examples:

- Can you tell me more about the day-to-day responsibilities of the position?
- How soon are you looking to fill the position?
- What do you enjoy about working for the company?
- If I am hired and am successful in my position, what are the career development opportunities for someone who starts in this type of a position?

I've heard several versions of this last question. I've seen people with passion, energy and self-confidence who are ready to be "managers" or want to know how to advance. Wanting to advance can be a great asset. However, make sure that you ask the question in the right way. Let the employer know that you plan to focus on doing a good job first and that you have an understanding that "moving up" isn't just about time spent in a job, but performing well.

One of the questions I regularly get about the interview is about how to deal with salary issues. Unfortunately, there is no universal answer for how to deal with the salary issues. Every employer is different. Some are straightforward from the beginning and will give you a salary range so you have an idea throughout the process of the range the position offers. Others keep it very close to the vest until the very moment of making an offer. With such wide varieties, it's hard to give advice that will fit most employers. With that being said, I'm a believer in honesty. If salary is a big issue for you, I think its fair to ask for a salary range for the position if you are far enough in the interview stage to know you are a serious candidate.

Another area that is sometimes difficult to maneuver is when an employer asks what your salary expectations are or what you are currently making. I have the same advice here: be honest. Honesty can only help in these situations. If you find an employer is trying to trick you into giving a low answer about of what you expect to be paid for the job, maybe that isn't the best employer for you. Remember, you are interviewing not just to get the job but also to find out for yourself whether or not this is going to be right fit and/or career move for you. I'm not saying all employers who do this are bad employers, but it's a practice that almost always makes the candidate uncomfortable. I would advise that you can give an honest answer as to what you are making now or what you expect to make and add a comment that you would hope that you'd be in the mid- to high range of the position because of the education and experience you bring to the position. Or you can tell them what your current salary is, but that you aren't satisfied with that salary because you believe you bring more value than that salary reflects. Whatever your answer, be honest. Be professional.

Another area involving salary that comes up is for some entry-level positions in sales in sports. As of the publishing of this book, entry-level sales positions start lower than most college graduates expect. I often get asked about how to deal with these low offers when you believe you are worth so much more. My answer is this: focus on the opportunity. While the base pay may not be what you were hoping to make in your first job out of college, if you work hard, absorb the information and training, more than likely you will be successful and you will make enough in commissions that in a year you will laugh at the fact you were even concerned with the pay. The opportunity is there. Focus on that opportunity, not the base pay.

No matter what style of interview is used, my advice is the same: be yourself. Continue throughout the process, self-confident in your ability to explain yourself and your experiences. If you stick with that, regardless of the style, you will be consistent in your answers.

Follow Up

It is customary to send a thank you note after an interview. I was always more impressed by a hand written note because I knew it meant the person had to take some extra time to write and send it. However, I think in most situations email is acceptable. It just isn't as impressive. This will probably change as Gen Y becomes more involved on the employer side of the process and they are more familiar with electronic communication as professional communication.

Personally, I think a hand written note goes a long way to show your interest in the position. Writing a two line thank you on your iPhone in the parking lot after an interview shows more of a mere formality than truly being thankful for the interview. On the other hand, you want to keep your energies focused on doing things that will drive the employer to hire you and while a handwritten thank you note always impressed me, I can't say it ever was a driver for me to hire someone. It just made me think that they "get it" when it comes to professionalism and business communication.

Thank you note – example:

April 1, 2013

Dear Ms. Smith:

Thank you for taking time to interview me today for the position of Marketing Coordinator. I enjoyed learning more about ABC Company, the Marketing Department and the position. After meeting with you and Bob Smith, I am convinced that I have the skills necessary to do the job and to exceed your expectations. I appreciate your time and look forward to talking with you again in the future.

Thank you,

Mark Davis

-Chapter 9: What employers look for
beyond education, experience and skill-

"Ability is what you're capable of doing. Motivation determines
what you do. Attitude determines how well you do it."
-Lou Holtz

Whether employers specifically write down what they are looking
for in candidates, it is typically some variation of the following formula:

Successful candidate = education + experience + skill + person

Most employers don't write this down or even verbalize it. I believe
recruiting would be much simpler if we all did that. However, in some
way shape or form, this is what employers use to determine which
applicants are the best candidates for the job.

At the end of the day, though, employers are trying to find the
person who has the "IT" factor or they are trying to find the "right fit"
with their department and organization. But this "IT" factor and "right
fit" are difficult to ascertain.

Generally, if someone has gotten past résumé screening and phone
prescreening, chances are they have the education and experience to do
the job they are interviewing for. So, what is it that employers are really
looking for in an interview? In reality, what most employers are looking
for are some sense of the traits and behaviors of a candidate. They want
to know how you are going to contribute to the company's overall goals
and success and how will you contribute to the bottom line. This often
depends more on the type of person you are rather than the jobs you've
held in the past.

The Person

The Person aspect of the equation is made up of the traits and
behaviors of the person. This is typically what an interview will try to
elicit from an applicant. Traits and behaviors are the best indicators of
whether a person can do the job. They are also the most difficult to
ascertain in an application process. Someone writing on their cover
letter or résumé that they are "energetic" or "determined" is fine, but an
employer is not going to take the applicant's word for it. They are going
to test them, meet with them, have others meet with them and so on to

figure out if the applicant really is the person the candidate seems to be in the interview.

Typical traits that employers look for in candidates are:
- **Positive Attitude**
- **Ability**
- **Intelligence**
- **Professionalism**
- **Maturity**
- **Confidence**
- **Self-motivation**
- **Self-accountable**
- **Self-disciplined**
- **Trustworthy**
- **Energetic**
- **Positive work ethic**
- **Sound judgment**
- **Coachable**
- **Passion**

Positive attitude

A positive attitude is at the top of this list for a reason. I have heard several hiring managers say that they will take positive attitude over experience any day of the week. I have heard managers say: "I can teach marketing. I can't teach a positive attitude". A person with a positive attitude is someone who doesn't get involved with workplace gossip, they see opportunity instead of negativity and they look for solutions rather than focus on the problem. Sports can be an up and down business. Wins and losses are felt throughout the organization. A positive attitude will get the person and those around them through difficult times.

Ability

The ability of someone to do the job has more than likely been assessed prior to the interview. The education and experience noted on the résumé will give the employer an idea of whether the candidate can do the job. However, in the interview, you will want to make it very clear that you qualify at the basic level of being able to do the job.

Intelligence

At its basic form, intelligence is the mental capability that involves the ability to reason, plan, solve problems, think abstractly, comprehend complex ideas, learn quickly and learn from experience.[5] There are a variety of reasons intelligence is important in considering a job applicant. An intelligent person will be able to learn the job quickly, understand business practices and typically be able to add value to a company by making processes more efficient and increase productivity. An intelligent person doesn't spend time being taught the same procedures over and over again, so that a manager can train a person once and then leave them to their work and more than likely add to their responsibilities as they catch on quickly.

Professionalism

Professionalism is the ability to handle situations in a business-like manner. This can be as simple as not texting while at work or receiving minimal personal calls. These are small things that show your supervisor that you can separate work from your personal life and that you understand work is important. Your attire may show your professionalism. The age-old advice is to "dress ahead," which means that you dress for the position ahead of you, even though you aren't in it. Professionalism can be shown by the manner in which you speak. In college, a very informal and casual manner of speaking is often appropriate. However, once you enter the workforce, you want to make sure that you don't sound like you're talking with your friends at a Friday night party. Your speech should be more deliberate and you should choose your words more carefully. Overall, professionalism is shown by creating a business-like image, communicating in a business-like manner and showing a business-like demeanor at work.

Maturity

Maturity is often shown by knowing how to behave in certain situations. Most clients and customers of the company you are applying with are mature adults. An employer wants to know that an employee is going to be able to interact professionally with those clients and fans. Business maturity is unrelated to the age of the person, but more related

---

[5] Linda S. Gottfredson, "Mainstream Science on Intelligence: An Editorial With 52 Signatories, History and Bibliography," *Wall Street Journal*, December 13, 1994.

to the ability to sit in a room with a high level executive, client or customer and present in a mature manner. A mature person is able to handle difficult situations without getting flustered. A mature person is guided by reason and not by emotion and acts appropriately in business situations.

Confidence

A person who believes in him or herself and their abilities is an extremely attractive quality to an employer. It is sometimes a difficult line to walk between confidence and arrogance. A confident person knows what he or she can do, but also knows what he or she cannot do and will do their best to learn in those areas. An arrogant person is one who believes they are better than everyone else. Arrogance can lead to mistakes, overconfidence and the inability to learn.

One of my favorite quotes from Katie Couric's "The Best Advice I Ever Got" is from David Calhoun, Chairman and CEO of the Nielsen Company who says, "Self-confidence is the most important characteristic of successful people. Self-confidence – a quiet self-confidence that is not cockiness, not conceit, not arrogance-is the key to excelling, no matter what you do in life."[6]

Self-motivated

A person who is self-motivated knows his/her purpose and his/her goals. They are someone who doesn't need a "carrot" dangled in front of them to succeed or hit goals. They have drive and determination. They will overcome obstacles and negativity. And they will do things without having to be asked. A self-motivated individual is proactive and finds solutions to problems without being asked. If you have the right people in the right positions with the right self-motivation, then a manager doesn't need to spend a lot of time managing. People will do what needs to be done to make the company successful without needing to constantly be told what to do or motivated to do a good job.

Also, people who are self-motivated take initiative. They ARE the answer. They find solutions. They see problems before they arise and they take steps to prevent them.

---

[6] Katie Couric. *The Best Advice I Ever Got. Lessons from Extraordinary Lives.* (New York: Random House, 2011), 21.

Self-accountable

A person who is self-accountable is someone who does not need someone else to lay out ground rules. They understand how to make good decisions based on their own high standards. A self-accountable person has high expectations of themselves and holds them self-accountable to those standards. They are someone who reviews their own work, is upset by mistakes they make (and accepts responsibility for those mistakes) and they learn from those mistakes to become a better employee.

Trustworthy

Trustworthiness can mean a variety of things, depending on the perspective. It can mean that you are someone who can be trusted to keep secret confidential situations, whether it involves money or information, company processes or procedures. It means that you can be a part of a confidential situation and those involved can trust you to keep that information to yourself. Also, trustworthiness is an important trait in leaders. A person leading a group needs to be trustworthy, not just in keeping confidences, but in general trustworthiness of being or leading– that you are fair, direct and consistent. Employees can trust you with their ideas, their work and more importantly, their careers.

Disciplined

A person who is disciplined is someone who is persistent, consistent and does things when or before they need done. A person who is disciplined doesn't procrastinate and will persevere regardless of obstacles. A disciplined person will do what is right regardless of how tired or frustrated you may be. They have schedules and routines and can be counted on because they impose their own regimens to get things done. A disciplined person plans for their success and follows through with hard work.

Energetic

Others are drawn to and inspired by energetic people. High-energy people get more done. Energy spurs creativity and teamwork. Certain positions require long hours and often interaction with the public. I've heard managers talk about "high energy" or "high capacity" – people who have the energy to get through long hours, difficult projects and come out on top at the end.

Positive work ethic

A person with a positive work ethic will do what needs to be done without supervision. They will come in early and work late. They will make the extra phone call at the end of the day or they will take work home at night to keep up on their workload. They will work through a lunch to get a project done. If there is downtime or they finish a project, they look for what they can do next or review a project to see what can be done better in the future. They know what needs to be done and they do it.

Positive work ethic isn't just about working long hours. It's also working smart. People who focus on the task at hand and finish it. They get things done. They can be counted on as the "go to" person in the department or company.

Sound judgment

Using sound judgment is such an important category that many employers use this category to evaluate employees in performance evaluations. A person who uses sound judgment can understand problems, come up with alternative solutions and choose a solution that solves the problem. Employers look for employees who can assess a situation and provide a solution that leads to success for the company. Whether an entry-level employee or a management level employee, it is important to the company to have employees who have the ability to solve problems.

Coachable

For many positions, having someone who is coachable is necessary. Employers often want someone who can learn quickly and is open to learning new ways of doing things. While employers are hopeful that a prospective employee brings some base knowledge or skills to a job, employers (especially those hiring entry-level positions) are often looking for people who are willing to learn the "company way." Many companies have a system of how to do things – accounting, sales, prospecting, and data-entry – that has some proven success. They want candidates who can quickly learn the "company way" and who are willing to do things the "company way."

Passion

Passion attracts passion. Passion leads people. Passion for excellence. Passion for sales. Passion for marketing. Passion for finance. Employers want employees to have a passion for what they do. Don't confuse this with being a passionate fan. Many sports teams assume the people working there are somewhat fans of the game, but most don't want the front office staff showing up in a ball cap and jersey to work. Front offices are not looking for super-fans to fill the ranks of accountant or marketing manager. The passion that employers look for is a passion for the job for which they are applying.

Your Brand

Basically, what this chapter all boils down to is this: What is your brand? What characteristics describe your personality, your outside of education and your experience? Who are you?

For most employers, they are looking for someone with most or all of the above-listed qualities. Often, the importance of the factors changes based on the type of job the person is applying for. For example, a hiring manager looking to hire a person in the finance department might be looking more for intelligence and trustworthiness and less for enthusiasm and energy.

I think Joe Leccese, Chairman of Proskauer Rose, LLP and co-head of the law firm's sports group, said it really well: "The notion of the one-size-fits-all interview probably leads to 90 percent bad interviews ... We have our best success with what one might call the renaissance man or renaissance woman." [7]   In other words, they are looking for people who are well rounded and have several of the positive characteristics listed above.

You need to come up with your brand. In a nutshell, who are you professionally? Here are some examples of personal brands:

"I am a hard working, aggressive college graduate who has a passion for sales and the sport industry. I get satisfaction from working hard, making phone calls, and creating relationships that lead to others' enjoyment of our team's events. When I stand in the bowl at the start of a game and feel the crowd's energy, I am excited that I was a small part of that."

---

[7] "Sit-Down with Joe Leccese," *Street & Smith's SportsBusiness Journal*, April 30-May 6, 2012, page 34.

"I am an intelligent, professional, and energetic college graduate. I am looking to find a job in the sport industry. I have worked on two marketing campaigns during my college internships and I believe that my education, experience and energy will be a tremendous addition to your marketing department."

"I am energy. I am up early and go to bed late. I strive for perfection and I consistently exceed the high goals I set for myself. I know what I need to do to reach my ultimate goals and I have lofty expectations of myself for success. I work hard at the job I'm in, but I look forward to the opportunities that lie ahead for me."

Some people refer to this brand statement as your "elevator pitch" or your 30-second personal statement. Whatever you want to call it, you should have one. This can be used at the end of the interview when you're asked to summarize yourself or when you are at a career fair introducing yourself to potential employers or as you network and meet new people.

All in all, employers are looking to see whether the candidate will make the company better for having been a part of it. Most employers know that the person being hired may only be with the company for a few years. While many employers hire with the thought that the employee will remain with the company for years, for some that isn't the case. Part of what employers in sports look for is whether the person will make a positive contribution during their time with the company. Whether it is generating revenue, restructuring department procedures or simply doing a very good job while they are employed, it is important that the person will be a positive influence on the company, whether it is for six months or 20 years. Your job in the interview is to show them that you are that person who not only fits the bill of the open position, but who will make the company better for having brought you on board.

-Epilogue: Prepare for Opportunity-

"I'm not telling you it's going to be easy.
I'm telling you it's going to be worth it."
-Art Williams

I started this book with the following premise:

What gets you an interview ...
  · **a professional, concise résumé**
  · **that outlines your experience**
  · **that matches the open position requirements and**
  · **outweighs the other candidates who have applied for the position.**

You may have noticed that this book focuses mainly on the first three parts of this equation. I have given you specific advice and examples on how to develop a professional, concise résumé. I also have given you advice on how to outline your experience in your résumé and cover letter. I have shown you how to write a cover letter and match up the open position requirements with your education and experience. But we really haven't touched on that last part. The reason for this is that, as an applicant, you have no control over that last part of the equation. It is equally as important as the others in your chances at landing a job, but you have no control over it. This is the part of the equation that many applicants don't understand.

First, you have no control over who and how many applicants are competing with you for a position. Second, you have no control over the qualifications of those applicants. You cannot spend a lot of time worrying about things you cannot control. So, you shouldn't spend too much time on the last part of the equation, but you do need to keep it in mind as you apply for jobs. You may have mastered everything in the job application process, but if there are better-qualified candidates out there, you aren't going to get the job (or even the interview). The best thing you can do is to keep at it. Do your best. Get the best education and experience that you can and do your best to stand out as a professional, intelligent job applicant. Don't get frustrated or disappointed if you aren't getting calls immediately after you have fine-tuned your application process. There are still a lot of unknowns and uncontrollable out there. But don't give up. The opportunities are out there.

After you've created your résumé, your cover letter, your network, your references and prepared for your interview (it will happen) ... ask yourself this question: If you were the person reviewing applicants, would you call yourself for an interview? If so, you're ready. If not, ask yourself what's missing and rework your résumé and cover letter.

I will finish with a few key tips and reminders:

- Write your own résumé. If you can't write your own résumé, how are you going to succeed in an interview? If you can't summarize yourself in a page or two, how are you going to spend 30 minutes, 2 hours or a half-day (depending on the process) interviewing for a position?
- Employers are looking for applicants who show a promise of intelligence and an ability to communicate professionally. That is why the detail of a résumé and cover letter matter.
- Focus on the employer's needs, not your desire to work in sports.
- Working in sports is fun. But it is also a business. Be professional. Be prepared.
- In sports, it's what you know AND who you know. Networking is important.
- Develop your brand. Developing a solid résumé and cover letter will help you come up with a solid 30-second brand statement or elevator pitch.

Remember that your success depends on you. It is up to you to prepare for the opportunities that lie ahead. Good luck!

"If opportunity doesn't knock, build a door."
Milton Berle

APPENDIX A: Step-by-Step Résumé

1. Copy the résumé included in this book – exactly as it is – on your computer. Bold where it is bold. Italicize where it is italicized.

2. Enter your basic information – name, address, educational institution, employers, job titles, dates, etc. over the template information. Start with the most recent job first and work backwards chronologically.

3. List your job responsibilities.

4. List any achievements or awards that were not specifically listed with a position. This is very important for students or recent college graduates who may not have much work experience.

5. Fill in the rest of the résumé – awards/distinctions, skills, activities.

APPENDIX B: Step-by-Step Cover Letter

1. Read the job posting.

2. Make a list of the qualifications and experience the employer is looking for in a candidate.

3. Next to the list of qualifications, write the experience you have that matches the listed item.

4. Draft an introductory paragraph. This paragraph should be a brief summary of what position you are applying for and a brief summary of your qualifications. See below for examples.

5. The middle paragraph or two should provide a detailed description of how your experience matches the qualifications sought for the position.

6. The final paragraph should summarize your education and experience and why you are a good candidate for the open position.

APPENDIX C: Interview Outline

I. Educational History
    A. Undergraduate education
        1. Major:
            a. Classes taken, short description and how class might relate to position interviewing for
        2. Minor:
            a. Classes taken, short description and how class might relate to position interviewing for
        3. Why I chose this area of study
        4. What types of positions this area of study prepared me for
    B. Graduate education
        1. Focus of study (MBA, MSA, J.D., PhD)
            a. Classes taken, short description and how class might relate to position interviewing for
        2. Why I chose this area of study
        3. What types of positions this area of study prepared me for
        4. What thesis or research work I did during my graduate studies.
        5. Special projects completed
II. RÉSUMÉ (Have a copy with you)
    A. Work History (including internships)
        1. Position with Company
            a. Responsibilities
            b. Responsibilities
            c. Achievements
            d. How this experience is relevant/beneficial to position interviewing for
    B. Activities
    C. Awards/Distinctions
III. Career Goals
    A. Short Term
    B. Long Term
IV. Summary statement of why you are the best candidate for the job

APPENDIX D: Recommended Resources

Career Services

University Career Services departments are underutilized. Use the services that are available to you as students.

Books – Sport, Sports Career and Career Related

- *The Comprehensive Guide to Careers in Sports.* Glenn Wong.
- *A career in sports: Advice from sports business leaders.* Wells, Kreutzer, Kahler.
- *Inside the Minds: The Business of Sports.* (2004). United States of America: Aspatore Books.
- *Sports Leaders & Success. 55 Top Sports Leaders & How They Achieved Greatness.* William J. O'Neil.
- *Moneyball: The Art of Winning an Unfair Game.* Michael Lewis. This was recently made into a high profile movie, but this book really does give you a good look at the inside of sports as a business.
- *What Color is Your Parachute? A Practical Manual for Job-Hunters and Career-Changers.* Richard Nelson Bolles.

Books –Leadership, Self-improvement

- Anything by John C. Maxwell. He is an excellent author on leadership principles that apply to all levels of employment and management. My favorites are: *25 Ways to Win with People* and *Today Matters*, but every book I have read of his is insightful, intelligent and can truly have an impact on your success.
- Anything by Pat Williams. His books on leadership are insightful and provide useful tools to make you a better leader, manager, employee, and/or teammate.
- *The 7 Habits of Highly Effective People.* Steven R. Covey.
- *Good to great: Why some companies make the leap – and others don't.* James Collins.
- *The Business of Happiness.* Ted Leonsis.
- *Winning.* Jack Welch.
- *The Best Advice I Ever Got. Lessons from Extraordinary Lives.* Katie Couric.
- *Our Golden Rule.* John H. McConnell.

Books – Grammar
- *The McGraw-Hill Handbook of English Grammar and Usage.* Mark Lester and Larry Beason.
- *Eats, Shoots & Leaves.* Lynn Truss.

Following is a small sample to get you started in what tools are available to you on the Internet. This is just to get you started. There are several other companies and websites that are available with excellent job postings and career advice.

General Job/Career Websites:

www.monster.com
www.careerbuilder.com
www.simplyhired.com
www.indeed.com (this is a site that pulls postings from other sites. Employers don't actually post on indeed.com so watch out to make sure that postings are up to date. Otherwise, it is a great site).

Job/Career Websites, specific to the Sport Industry:

www.teamworkonline.com
www.workinsports.com
www.jobsinsports.com
www.womensportsjobs.com
www.espncareers.com
www.sportsearchonline.com
www.thesportsresume.com

Website with information on getting a degree (undergraduate and/or graduate) in Sport Management/Sport Administration:

www.degreesinsports.com

Also, there are some great resources to follow on Twitter:

@workinsports
@teamworkonline

@jobsinsports
@breakintosports
@sportsjobfinder
@socialhire.com
@dreamcareersinc
@elitecareers1
@sportscareers
@espncareers
@simplyhired
@TheSportsResume
@sportsearch
@careerbuilder

Most of the above Twitter accounts are specific to those looking for jobs in sports, but there are also a couple of resources out there that aren't specific to sports, but have a great amount of knowledge and advice for college students as they transition into their careers. My favorites are:

@hrlegalconsult (that's my Twitter account)
@lindsaypollak
@greatonthejob

And teams, leagues, conferences, and other sport related entities have their own websites, such as:

www.nfl.com
www.nba.com
www.mlb.com
www.nhl.com
www.mls.com
www.nascar.com
www.ncaa.com
www.bigten.org
www.mac-sports.com
www.themwc.com
www.secdigitalnetwork.com

APPENDIX E: Sample Résumé Styles

The following résumés are the exact same résumé in detail. Only the formatting is changed. Format can be important in that it catches the eye of the reader and makes it easy for the reader to compare your education and skill against others. Do not overdo formatting, unless you are applying for a job where the skill of design is important. Remember – it's about showcasing your education, experience and skill, not your ability to come up with fancy fonts.

The examples to follow have smaller fonts than I would normally recommend, but this is done to show you what the example would look like on one page, these are not the templates that you should use to copy. These are to show you the difference in appearance by using different fonts and formats.

Mark Davis
123 Elm Street
Springfield, US 12345

(555) 555-5555
mdavis@email.com

Education:
University of Studies
Bachelor's Degree in Sport Management
Anticipated Graduation Date May 2013
3.7 GPA

Relevant Coursework:

Business Law	Intro to Sport Management	Sport Marketing
Marketing	Accounting	Business Operations

Experience:

LMNO Company
Intern   May – August 2012
- Responsible for game day preparations, including message boards and group events
- Cold called potential customers to sell single game tickets
- Assisted with preparation and implementation of game day promotions

XYZ Company
Marketing Intern   May – August, 2011
- Organized sales lead system, including inputting and sorting information in marketing database
- Conducted market research on local college campuses regarding a new product line
- Compiled research information and presented a report to Marketing Department that highlighted market research and recommendations for college campus launch of new product line

Achievements/Awards:
- Dean's List at University of Studies, Fall 2010 – Spring 2013
- Presidential Scholarship Recipient 2012, 2013

Activities:
- Alpha Alpha Alpha Honorary Society
  - Vice President 2012-2013
  - Member 2010-2013
- Varsity Soccer Team, University of Studies
  - Captain 2012
  - Team Member 2010-2013

Mark Davis
123 Elm Street
Springfield, US 12345
(555) 555-5555
mdavis@email.com

Education:
University of Studies
Bachelor's Degree in Sport Management
Anticipated Graduation Date May 2013
3.7 GPA

Experience:
LMNO Company
Intern
May – August 2012
Responsible for game day preparations, including message boards and group events. Cold called potential customers to sell single game tickets. Assisted with preparation and implementation of game day promotions

XYZ Company
Marketing Intern
May – August, 2011
Organized sales lead system, including inputting and sorting information in marketing database. Conducted market research on local college campuses regarding a new product line. Compiled research information and presented a report to Marketing Department that highlighted market research and recommendations for college campus launch of new product line

Achievements/Awards:
Dean's List at University of Studies, Fall 2010 – Spring 2013
Presidential Scholarship Recipient 2012, 2013

Activities:
Alpha Alpha Alpha Honorary Society (Vice President 2012-2013,
    Member 2010-2013)
Varsity Soccer Team, University of Studies (Captain 2012, Team
    Member 2010-2013)

Mark Davis
123 Elm Street
Springfield, US 12345
(555) 555-5555
mdavis@email.com

Education:
University of Studies
Bachelor's Degree in Sport Management
Anticipated Graduation Date May 2013
3.7 GPA

Experience:
LMNO Company
Intern
May – August 2012

- Responsible for game day preparations, including message boards and group events
- Cold called potential customers to sell single game tickets
- Assisted with preparation and implementation of game day promotions

XYZ Company
Marketing Intern
May – August, 2011

- Organized sales lead system, including inputting and sorting information in marketing database
- Conducted market research on local college campuses regarding a new product line
- Compiled research information and presented a report to Marketing Department that highlighted market research and recommendations for college campus launch of new product line

Achievements/Awards:
- Dean's List at University of Studies, Fall 2010 – Spring 2013
- Presidential Scholarship Recipient 2012, 2013

Activities:
- Alpha Alpha Alpha Honorary Society
  - Vice President 2012-2013
  - Member 2010-2013
- Varsity Soccer Team, University of Studies
  - Captain 2012
  - Team Member 2010-2013

Mark Davis

123 Elm Street
Springfield, US 12345

(555) 555-5555
mdavis@email.com

Education:

University of Studies
Bachelor's Degree in Sport Management
Anticipated Graduation Date May 2013
3.7 GPA

Experience:

LMNO Company
Intern
May – August 2012

- Responsible for game day preparations, including message boards and group events
- Cold called potential customers to sell single game tickets
- Assisted with preparation and implementation of game day promotions

XYZ Company
Marketing Intern
May – August, 2011

- Organized sales lead system, including inputting and sorting information in marketing database
- Conducted market research on local college campuses regarding a new product line
- Compiled research information and presented a report to Marketing Department that highlighted market research and recommendations for college campus launch of new product line

Achievements/Awards:

- Dean's List at University of Studies, Fall 2010 – Spring 2013
- Presidential Scholarship Recipient 2012, 2013

Activities:

- Alpha Alpha Alpha Honorary Society
  - Vice President 2012-2013
  - Member 2010-2013
- Varsity Soccer Team, University of Studies
  - Captain 2012
  - Team Member 2010-2013

Skills:

- Proficient in Microsoft Office (Word, Excel, Power Point, Outlook), Internet Research, and Adobe Acrobat.

Acknowledgements

To my family– Team Walton – Bill, Luke & Ryan; my late father; my mom and stepdad, my brothers, my in-laws, and to all of my friends and family – Kaufmans, Waltons, and Crouches (and especially the fantastic Crouch Editing Team)– your support throughout my life, career, career changes and writing this book is instrumental to where I am today. *Thank you!*

To my Ohio University family – there is no question why you are THE ONE. I'm honored to be a part of your incredible team.

To my Columbus Blue Jackets family – from that incredibly special inaugural year to today, I am thankful for the incredible people that I was privileged to work with and the tremendous experience I had with each of you. A special thank you to Chrissie Parthemore, who for seven years was by my side as the CBJ Fun Police. Your friendship and support is immeasurable. A special thank you to my mentor, friend, colleague, ex-boss, recommender of excellent interns, etc. – Greg Kirstein. You always believed in me. Thank you doesn't seem enough. I wish more people had strong, intelligent and kind guiding forces in their lives.

To my Capital University family – thank you for the opportunity to teach and for such incredible support as I made a complete change in my career. A special thank you to 2013 grads Jordan Helmer and Skylar Prange for your assistance with this book. You are both the epitome of professional, intelligent and hard working students.

Finally, a special thank you to the Northwest Library in Worthington and Capital University Blackmore Library and their staff for quick and courteous service and for always having a nice, quiet space for me.

ABOUT THE AUTHOR

Kelley Walton is a Consultant, specializing in Career Consulting and Human Resources Consulting in the Sport Industry. She has a bachelor's degree in Interpersonal Communications from Eastern Michigan University and a Juris Doctor Degree from Capital University Law School. She has over ten years of experience working in professional sports and is the former Director of Human Resources for the Columbus Blue Jackets.

At the time of publication, Ms. Walton is also an Adjunct Professor at Ohio University in the Department of Sports Administration, an Adjunct Professor at Capital University and practices law on a part-time basis.

www.kwaltonconsulting.com

Follow on Twitter @hrlegalconsult